faith first

Legacy Edition
PARISH

Grade One

RCL✻
Benziger®

Cincinnati, Ohio

"The Ad Hoc Committee to Oversee the Use of the Catechism, United States Conference of Catholic Bishops, has found this catechetical series, copyright 2006, to be in conformity with the *Catechism of the Catholic Church*."

NIHIL OBSTAT
Reverend Robert M. Coerver
Censor Librorum

IMPRIMATUR
† Most Rev. Charles V. Grahmann
Bishop of Dallas

September 15, 2004

The Nihil Obstat and Imprimatur are official declarations that the material reviewed is free of doctrinal or moral error. No implication is contained therein that those granting the Nihil Obstat and Imprimatur agree with the contents, opinions, or statements expressed.

Send all inquiries to:
RCL Benziger
8805 Governor's Hill Drive
Suite 400
Cincinnati, Ohio 45249

Toll Free   877-275-4725
Fax   800-688-8356

Visit us at www.RCLBenziger.com
            www.FaithFirst.com

Printed in the United States of America

20471   ISBN 978-0-7829-1063-6 (Student Book)
20481   ISBN 978-0-7829-1075-9 (Catechist Guide)

9th Printing.
March 2015.

ACKNOWLEDGMENTS

Scripture excerpts are taken or adapted from the *New American Bible with Revised New Testament and Psalms,* copyright © 1991, 1986, 1970, Confraternity of Christian Doctrine, Washington, DC. Used with permission. All rights reserved. No part of the *New American Bible* may be reproduced by any means without the permission of the copyright owner.

Excerpts are taken or adapted from the English translation of *Rite of Baptism for Children* © 1969, International Committee on English in the Liturgy, Inc. (ICEL); the English translation of *The Roman Missal* © 2010, ICEL; the English translation of *Rite of Confirmation, Second Edition* © 1975, ICEL; the English translation of the Act of Contrition from *Rite of Penance* © 1974, ICEL the English translation of *A Book of Prayers* © 1982, ICEL; the English translation of *Book of Blessings* © 1987, ICEL; *Catholic Household Blessings and Prayers* (revised edition) © 2007, United States Conference of Catholic Bishops, Washington, D.C. Used with permission. All rights reserved.

Excerpts are taken or adapted from the English translation of the *Apostles' Creed* and the *Gloria Patri* by the International Consultation on English Texts (ICET).

Faith First Legacy Edition
Development Team

Developing a religion program requires the gifts and talents of many individuals working together as a team. RCL Benziger is proud to acknowledge the contributions of these dedicated people.

Program Theology Consultants
Reverend Louis J. Cameli, S.T.D.
Reverend Robert D. Duggan, S.T.D.

Advisory Board
Judith Deckers, M.Ed.
Elaine McCarron, SCN, M.Div.
Marina Herrera, Ph.D.
Reverend Frank McNulty, S.T.D.
Reverend Ronald J. Nuzzi, Ph.D.

National Catechetical Advisor
Jacquie Jambor

Catechetical Specialist
Jo Rotunno

Contributing Writers
Student Book and Catechist Guide
Christina DeCamp
Judith Deckers
Mary Beth Jambor
Marianne K. Lenihan
Michele Norfleet

Art & Design Director
Lisa Brent

Electronic Page Makeup
Laura Fremder

Production Director
Jenna Nelson

Designers/Photo Research
Pat Bracken
Kristy O. Howard
Susan Smith

Project Editors
Patricia A. Classick
Steven M. Ellair
Ronald C. Lamping

Web Site Producers
Joseph Crisalli
Demere Henson

General Editor
Ed DeStefano

President/Publisher
Maryann Nead

Contents

WELCOME TO FAITH FIRST7

Unit 1—We Believe

GETTING READY 12

CHAPTER 1   God Loves Us 13
Faith concepts: The gift of faith, Abraham and Sarah, Jesus, the gift of family, the Catholic Church, the Sign of the Cross
Scripture: Genesis 17:4, 15–16
Prayer: The Sign of the Cross

CHAPTER 2   God Is Our Father and Creator 21
Faith concepts: God the Father and Creator, created in God's image, images of God, caring for God's world, the Our Father
Scripture: Genesis 1:31, Genesis 1:26–31, Luke 11:2, Psalm 148
Prayer: Thank you prayer

CHAPTER 3   Jesus Is the Son of God 29
Faith concepts: The Birth of Jesus; Jesus the Son of God; the Holy Family; Mary the Mother of Jesus; Joseph; sharing God's love; the Lord, have mercy
Scripture: Luke 2:15–17, 20
Prayer: An act of love

CHAPTER 4   Mary Is the Mother of God: A Scripture Story 37
Faith concepts: Mary the Mother of God, the Bible, angels, faith and trust, honoring Mary
Scripture: Luke 1:28, 31, 35, 38; Psalm 1:1–2
Prayer: Praying a Psalm

CHAPTER 5   Jesus Shows God's Love . . . 45
Faith concepts: The Crucifixion, the Resurrection, the Ascension, the women disciples of Jesus, the Easter candle
Scripture: Luke 24:1–4, 6; Matthew 28:7
Prayer: Praying a litany

CHAPTER 6   The Good Samaritan: A Scripture Story 53
Faith concepts: The Bible, the Old Testament, the New Testament, the Gospels, being good neighbors, Catholic hospitals
Scripture: Luke 10:30, 33–35
Prayer: A prayer of the faithful

CHAPTER 7   The Holy Spirit Is Our Helper 61
Faith concepts: The Holy Trinity, the Holy Spirit, Jesus' promise to send the Holy Spirit, the Holy Spirit as helper, signs of the Holy Spirit
Scripture: John 14:16, John 13:34
Prayer: A prayer to the Holy Spirit

CHAPTER 8   Jesus Gave Us the Church . . . 69
Faith concepts: The Church as the People of God, the Catholic Church, the Church as community, the saints, Mary the greatest saint, Saint Peter the Apostle
Scripture: Acts of the Apostles 2:1–4
Prayer: Litany of the Saints

CHAPTER 9   The First Christians Follow Jesus: A Scripture Story 77
Faith concepts: Christians, the early Church, living as a Christian, patron saints
Scripture: Acts of the Apostles 2:42, 45–47
Prayer: The Sign of Peace

UNIT 1—REVIEW 85

Unit 2—We Worship

GETTING READY 88

CHAPTER 10   The Church Celebrates All Year 89
Faith concepts: The Church's year of worship, Advent, Christmas, Lent, Easter, Ordinary Time, celebrating Sunday
Scripture: Psalm 150
Prayer: A prayer of praise

CHAPTER 11   The Church's Celebrations . . . 97
Faith concepts: Sacraments, Celebrating Baptism, Adam and Eve, original sin, Celebrating Confirmation, living our Baptism
Scripture: Matthew 5:14–16
Prayer: A prayer of thanks

CHAPTER 12   Come, Follow Jesus: A Scripture Story 105
Faith concepts: The Gospel, Good News of God's love, the work of the disciples, growing in faith
Scripture: Matthew 28:19–20
Prayer: Signing a prayer

CHAPTER 13 **We Celebrate Mass** 113
Faith concepts: The Mass, listening to God's
word at Mass, the Last Supper,
celebrating the Eucharist, Holy
Communion, loving and serving the Lord
Scripture: Matthew 26:26–28; Matthew 5:9
Prayer: A prayer of thanksgiving, praying
quietly and praying aloud

CHAPTER 14 **Jesus Feeds a Crowd:**
A Scripture Story 121
Faith concepts: Galilee, the people of Jesus'
time, Jesus feeds a crowd, miracles, God's
gift of grace
Scripture: Matthew 14:15–16, 19–20
Prayer: A blessing prayer

UNIT 2—REVIEW 129

Unit 3–We Live

GETTING READY 132

CHAPTER 15 **We Live as**
Children of God 133
Faith concepts: Children of God, creation of
people as images of God, the gift of life,
respecting and caring for life, giving glory
to God, heaven, the Blessed Sacrament
Scripture: Genesis 1:27
Prayer: The Glory Prayer

CHAPTER 16 **We Live as a Family** 141
Faith concepts: Marriage, the sacrament of
Matrimony, Christian families, the Holy
Family, the family church
Scripture: Luke 2:41–52
Prayer: A family blessing

CHAPTER 17 **We Live as a Community** . . . 149
Faith concepts: Living in a community, rules
and laws, the Great Commandment,
religious communities
Scripture: Psalm 25:4 and 5
Prayer: Praying the Bible

CHAPTER 18 **Moses Leads God's People:**
A Scripture Story 157
Faith concepts: Moses, manna in the desert,
God's caring love for his people
Scripture: Exodus 15:22, 24; 16:2–4, 13–16
Prayer: A vocation prayer

CHAPTER 19 **We Love God** 165
Faith concepts: The Ten Commandments,
the new commandment of Jesus,
worshiping God, First Commandment,
Second Commandment, Third
Commandment, churches
Scripture: John 13:34
Prayer: An act of love

CHAPTER 20 **We Love Others** 173
Faith concepts: The Fourth through the
Tenth Commandments, respecting others
and what belongs to them, honesty and
truthfulness
Scripture: Acts of the Apostles 2:42–47
Prayer: A prayer of intercession

CHAPTER 21 **We Love Through**
Forgiveness 181
Faith concepts: Making choices, sin, sorrow
for sin, asking for forgiveness, forgiving
others, sign of peace
Scripture: Matthew 18:21–22
Prayer: A prayer of mercy

CHAPTER 22 **Jesus and the Children:**
A Scripture Story 189
Faith concepts: the kingdom of God, heaven,
children of God
Scripture: Mark 10:13–14, 16
Prayer: A prayer of meditation, or guided
imagery

UNIT 3—REVIEW 197

Unit 4–We Pray

GETTING READY 200

CHAPTER 23 **We Talk and Listen to God** . . 201
Faith concepts: Prayer, the Holy Spirit and
prayer, the prayer of Jesus, prayer
partners
Scripture: Matthew 7:7–11
Prayer: The Hail Mary

CHAPTER 24 **Jesus Teaches His Followers**
to Pray: A Scripture Story . . . 209
Faith concepts: Praying for ourselves and for
others, trusting that God hears our
prayers, praying with people in our
community
Scripture: Matthew 6:7
Prayer: A simple prayer

CHAPTER 25 **We Pray in Many Ways** 217
Faith concepts: Praying with words and
actions, praying psalm and hymns, sacred
music
Scripture: Psalm 150:2–3, 6
Prayer: Praying with actions

CHAPTER 26 **Jesus Teaches Us the**
Our Father: A Scripture Story . . 225
Faith concepts: The Our Father, the parts of
the Our Father
Scripture: Matthew 6:9–13
Prayer: The Our Father

UNIT 4—REVIEW 233

We Celebrate: The Liturgical Seasons

THE LITURGICAL YEAR 236
The seasons of the Church's year

ORDINARY TIME 237
The Church's year, liturgical colors,
Ordinary Time

THE SEASON OF ADVENT
The First Week of Advent. Preparing
to celebrate Christmas, Christians as
lights for the world 239
The Second Week of Advent. The work
of Saint John the Baptist 241
The Third Week of Advent. The
announcement to Mary that she would
be the mother of Jesus, Mary's visit
to Elizabeth 243
The Fourth Week of Advent. The
promise of Micah the Prophet,
preparing to welcome Jesus the Savior . . . 245

THE SEASON OF CHRISTMAS
Christmas. The birth of Jesus, the angels'
announcement to the shepherds,
the shepherds' response 247
Epiphany. The visit of the Magi 249

THE SEASON OF LENT
The First Week of Lent. Preparing
for Easter, a time to grow in faith
and love 251
The Second Week of Lent. A special
time of prayer 253
The Third Week of Lent. Making good
choices, a time of forgiveness and making
peace 255
The Fourth Week of Lent. A time for
giving and sharing. 257
The Fifth Week of Lent. A time of
forgiveness 259

HOLY WEEK
Palm Sunday of the Lord's Passion.
Jesus' final entry into Jerusalem. 261
Holy Thursday/Triduum. The Last
Supper, celebrating the Eucharist. 263

Good Friday/Triduum. Remembering
Jesus' suffering and death, venerating
the cross 265
Easter/Triduum. New life, Easter people,
Alleluia, Sunday as a little Easter 267

THE SEASON OF EASTER
The Second Week of Easter. The
Resurrection of Jesus, Mary
Magdalene, Thomas the Apostle 269
The Third Week of Easter. The vine
and the branches 271
The Fourth Week of Easter. Proclaiming
the Good News of Jesus. 273
The Fifth Week of Easter. Life in the
early Church. 275
The Sixth Week of Easter. Jesus the
Good Shepherd, Peter the Apostle 277
The Seventh Week of Easter.
The Ascension. 279
Pentecost. The work of the Holy Spirit
in the Church 281

CATHOLIC PRAYERS AND PRACTICES 283

WE CELEBRATE THE MASS 289

A TOUR OF THE CHURCH 292

GLOSSARY 294

INDEX 302

CREDITS 304

Welcome to Faith First!

We Pray

Loving God,
we are happy to be in
first grade.
We will learn about you
and your Son, Jesus.
Help us to learn how
much you love us.
Help us to show our
love for you.
Amen.

My Favorites

Tell a friend about some of your favorite things.

- Animal
- Food
- Holiday
- Game
- Bible story

All About Me

My name is

_____

- -

_____

I am a child of God.

✝ F A I T H

We will learn new things this year about God at church and at home.

1. We Believe

We will learn about God's Son, Jesus.

Look on page 31. Find out the name of Jesus' mother. Trace her name on the line.

Mary

2. We Celebrate

We will learn how our Church celebrates all year long.

Look on page 114. Learn the name of the most important celebration of the Church. Trace the word under the picture.

Mass

FIRST ✝

3. We Live

We will learn how to be good followers of Jesus.

Look on page 184. Learn one good thing to do. Trace the word under the picture.

Forgive

4. We Pray

We will learn how to talk and listen to God.

Look on page 203. Learn who teaches us how to pray. Trace the name under the picture.

Jesus

The Word of the Lord

LEADER: We gather to praise your word, O Lord.

ALL: Happy are the people who listen to God's word.

LEADER: A reading from the book of the prophet Isaiah.
Just as rain and snow come down and water the earth,
So shall my word come down and do my will.
My word will bring you peace and joy.

Based on Isaiah 51:10–12

The word of the Lord.

ALL: Thanks be to God.

LEADER: Come forward and bow before the Bible.

What does the Church
ask us to believe?

Getting Ready

What I Have Learned

What is something you already know about these faith words?

God

_____

- - - - - - - - - - - - - - - - - -

_____

Jesus

_____

- - - - - - - - - - - - - - - - - -

_____

The Holy Spirit

_____

- - - - - - - - - - - - - - - - - -

_____

Words to Know

Put an X next to the faith words you know. Put a ? next to the faith words you need to know more about.

Faith Words

_____ faith

_____ Creator

_____ Bible

_____ Holy Spirit

_____ Catholic

_____ Church

A Question I Have

What question would you like to ask about God?

_____

- - - - - - - - - - - - - - - - - -

_____

_____

- - - - - - - - - - - - - - - - - -

_____

From a Scripture Story

Mary and the angel

What message did the angel give to Mary?

God Loves Us

We Pray

Lord God, we believe in you. We hope in you. We love you. Amen.

Who knows and loves you?

God knows and loves all people. God wants us to know and love him too.

Who helps you to know and love God?

Faith Focus

Who helps us to know God and to believe in him?

Faith Words

believe
> *Believe* means to have faith in God. It means to give ourselves to God with all our heart.

faith
> Faith is a gift from God. It helps us to know God and to believe in God.

The Gift of Faith

God knows us very well. He loves us all the time. God wants us to know and love him too.

Abraham and Sarah were friends of God. They lived a long time ago. They lived before Jesus was born. God chose Abraham to be a great leader. God made a promise to Abraham. He said,

"You will be the father of many nations. I will bless you and your wife Sarah. You will soon become the parents of a son."   Based on Genesis 17:4, 15–16

Abraham and Sarah came to **believe** God. They had **faith** in God and in his promises.

What did God promise Abraham?

14

Jesus Helps Us to Know God

Many years later, God sent Jesus to us. Jesus is the Son of God. Jesus helps us best to know God and his love. Jesus helps us to believe in God. Jesus helps us to have faith in God.

Jesus taught over and over again how much God loves us. He taught us that God is love.

Isaac

Isaac is the son of Abraham and Sarah. He is the son God promised Abraham and Sarah. The name *Isaac* means "he laughs." Isaac brought much joy to his parents.

ACTIVITY *Color the spaces with Xs one color and the spaces with Os other colors. Find out who teaches us the most about God.*

Our Family Helps Us

Jesus gave us the gift of a family. Our family helps us to know God and to believe in God.

Our family helps us to give ourselves to God with all our heart. Our family helps us to grow in faith.

 Trace the words. Discover one important thing about God.

God loves us

Our Church Makes a Difference

The Catholic Church

We belong to the Catholic Church. Our parish is our home in the Catholic Church. Our parish is our Church family. Our parish helps us to know and to believe in God. Our parish helps us to love and to serve God.

We pray together. We listen to the Bible. We learn about Jesus and God's love. We help each other, and other people help us.

 Look at the three pictures on this page. Which of these things do you do with your parish?

Our Catholic Faith

Sign of the Cross
Catholics pray the Sign of the Cross. This shows we have faith in God.

17

What Difference Does Faith Make in My Life?

Your family and the Church help you to believe in God and to love God. You can help your family and friends to believe in God and to love God too.

In one heart draw people helping you to believe in God. In the second heart draw yourself sharing God's love with someone.

Sharing God's Love

My Faith Choice

Check (✔) how you will show your love for God. This week I will

❑ tell others about God.

❑ thank God for his love.

Sign of the Cross

We pray the Sign of the Cross to show we believe in God. Learn to pray the Sign of the Cross. Pray it with your class.

"In the name of the Father,

and of the Son,

and of the Holy Spirit.

Amen."

We Remember

Complete the sentences. Color the ◯ next to the best choice.

1. _____ means to have faith in God.
   ◯ Believe   ◯ Hope

2. Faith is a gift from _____.
   ◯ our friends   ◯ God

To Help You Remember

1. God helps us to know and to believe in him.

2. Our family and our Church help us to know God and to believe in God.

3. Jesus, the Son of God, helps us best to know God and to have faith in God.

This Week . . .

In chapter 1, "God Loves Us," your child learned that God has revealed himself and invites us to believe in him. Jesus Christ revealed the most about God. He is the Son of God and the fullness of God's revelation. Our family and our Church help us grow in faith and in our knowledge and love of God.

For more on the teachings of the Catholic Church on the mystery of the gift of faith, see *Catechism of the Catholic Church* paragraph numbers 80–95 and 142–175.

Sharing God's Word

Read together the Bible story in Genesis 17:1–6 about God's promise to Abraham or read the adaptation of the story on page 14. Emphasize the faith of Abraham and Sarah.

Praying

In this chapter your child prayed the Sign of the Cross. This week begin and end your family prayers by praying the Sign of the Cross together.

Making a Difference

Choose one of the following activities to do as a family or design a similar activity of your own.

- This week when you take part in Mass as a family, stop at the baptismal font or holy water font. Bless yourselves with the water, praying the Sign of the Cross.

- Compile a list of the names of people who have helped or who are helping your family grow in faith. Have each family member send a thank-you note to one person on the list.

- Make a banner with the words "God Loves Us." Display the banner where it can serve as a constant reminder to the whole family.

For more ideas on ways your family can live your faith, visit the "Faith First for Families" page at **www.FaithFirst.com**. You will find the "About Your Child" page helpful as your child begins a new year.

God Is Our Father and Creator

We Pray

We believe in God the Creator of heaven and earth.   Amen.

What is your favorite part of creation?

The world is a wonderful place. It is God's gift to us.

What does your favorite part of creation tell you about God?

The World Tells Us About God

Faith Focus

What does creation tell us about God?

Faith Words

Creator
God is the Creator. God made everything out of love and without any help.

image of God
We are created in the image of God. We are children of God.

God Made the World

God is the **Creator.** God made the whole world. He is the Creator of heaven and earth. God made everything without any help. The Bible tells us,

> God looked at everything he made. He saw that it was very good. *Based on Genesis 1:31*

God the Creator made everything out of love. God is love. God shares his love with us forever.

Think of your favorite part of God's creation. Draw a picture of it. Share what it tells you about God.

God Created People

God is the Creator of all people. God created every person to be an **image of God.** In the Bible we read,

> God made people in his image. He blessed them and told them to take care of everything he made. God said everything he made was very good.   Based on Genesis 1:26–31

God loves every person. We are very special to God. God made us to be happy with him now and forever in heaven.

ACTIVITY *You are very special to God. Tell God he is very special to you.*

God Is Our Loving Father

God made people in the image of God. We are children of God. God the Creator is our loving Father.

Jesus helped us to know and believe that God is our Father. He taught us to pray,

Our Father in heaven, hallowed be your name.

Based on Luke 11:2

God the Father knows and loves us. Jesus told us that God the Father cares for all his creation. He especially cares for people.

We show we love God our Father when we take care of ourselves. We show our love for God when we take care of creation.

Check (✓) ways you show your love for God.

God Loves Me

- ☐ Clean up trash.
- ☐ Get enough sleep.
- ☐ Be kind to pets.
- ☐ Do my best in school.

I Love God

We Care for God's World

The people of Prince of Peace Catholic Parish show their love for God the Creator. They take good care of all God's gifts. They joined the "Adopt-a-Street" program in their town.

Families of the parish meet on the third Saturday of each month. They put on their bright orange vests. Each family gets a rake and a trash bag. The families go and pick up trash by the side of the road.

When they do this, they are taking care of creation. This shows their love for God.

QUESTION *What is one way you and your family can take care of creation?*

Our Catholic Faith

The Our Father

The Church prays the Our Father at every Mass. We tell God we love him. We tell God we know he loves and cares for us.

Adopt a Street
LITTER CONTROL
Prince of Peace
Catholic Parish

What Difference Does Faith Make in My Life?

God's world is God's gift of love to everybody. You show you love God when you take care of God's world.

In the first puzzle piece draw a picture of something in God's creation that needs care. In the second puzzle piece draw how you can take care of it.

I Take Care of God's World

My Faith Choice

 This week I will take care of God's creation. I will try to do what I have drawn in the puzzle.

Thank You, God!

A rebus prayer uses pictures. Use a word
for each picture. Pray the prayer together.

All: Thank you, God, for your ♥.

Reader 1: You made the 👧👧.

All: Thank you, God, for your ♥.

Reader 2: You made the ☀ and the 🌙.
You made all the shining ✨.

All: Thank you, God, for your ♥.

Reader 3: You made the ⛰, and the 🌳.

All: Thank you, God, for your ♥.
You made ME!

Based on Psalm 148

We Remember

Draw a line from the words in Column A to
the sentences they complete in Column B.

Column A   **Column B**

1. Jesus   **a.** ____ made everything
            out of love.

2. People   **b.** ____ taught us to call
            God our Father.

3. God   **c.** ____ are made in the
            image of God.

To Help You Remember

1. God is the Creator. He made the whole world out of love and without any help.

2. God created people in the image of God.

3. Jesus reminded us that God is our Father.

This Week . . .

In chapter 2, "God Is Our Father and Creator," your child explored God's revelation of himself as Creator and Father. Everything exists because God, out of love, created it. All God's creation is good. God created people with all their differences in his image and likeness. Every person has been created to be an image of God. Jesus revealed to us the depth of God's love by reminding us that God is our Father. God unconditionally loves and cares for all people. An important response to God the Creator's love is our care, or stewardship, of creation.

For more on the teachings of the Catholic Church on the mystery of God the Father and Creator, see *Catechism of the Catholic Church* paragraph numbers 232–248 and 268–314.

Sharing God's Word

Read together the Bible story in Genesis 1:26–31 about the creation of people or read the adaptation of the story on page 23. Emphasize that every person is an image of God.

Praying

In this chapter your child prayed a rebus prayer of thanksgiving. Pray the prayer on page 27 together.

Making a Difference

Choose one of the following activities to do as a family or design a similar activity of your own.

- God created each person out of love. Take turns sharing what you like about each person.

- Go for a walk outside and name the parts of creation you see or hear. Or look at picture books or photo albums and name the parts of creation you see. Thank God for the wonderful gift of his creation.

- Make a mural showing how members of your family are caring for creation.

For more ideas on ways your family can live your faith, visit the "Faith First for Families" page at **www.FaithFirst.com**. This week pay special attention to "Questions Kids Ask."

Jesus Is the Son of God

We Pray

Blessed be the name of Jesus now and for ever.

Amen.

When is your birthday?

Birthdays are wonderful days. The Bible tells us about the birthday of Jesus.

What do you know about the Bible story about the birth of Jesus?

Jesus Is Born

Faith Focus

Who is Jesus?

Faith Words

Son of God
Jesus is the Son of God. Jesus is truly God and truly man.

Holy Family
The Holy Family is the family of Jesus, Mary, and Joseph.

The Son of God

At Christmas each year we remember the birth of Jesus. Jesus is the **Son of God.** Jesus is truly God and truly man.

The shepherds rushed and found Mary, Joseph, and Jesus. They told everyone about Jesus and praised God for all they heard and saw.

Based on Luke 2:15–17, 20

ACTIVITY Look at the picture. Tell a partner what you see. Together give praise to God as the shepherds did.

The Holy Family

Mary is the mother of Jesus, the Son of God. Joseph is the foster father of Jesus. We call Jesus, Mary, and Joseph the **Holy Family.** The Holy Family lived in a town called Nazareth.

Mary and Joseph showed their love for Jesus. They took very good care of Jesus as he was growing up. Jesus grew in his love of God and of people.

 Draw a picture of how your family helps you to grow in your love for God.

My Family

Jesus Shares God's Love

When Jesus grew up, he taught others about God. He shared God's love with everyone.

Jesus showed us how to treat people. Jesus treated everyone with kindness and respect. Respect means to treat every person as a child of God.

We are to treat everyone with kindness and respect. We are to share God's love with people.

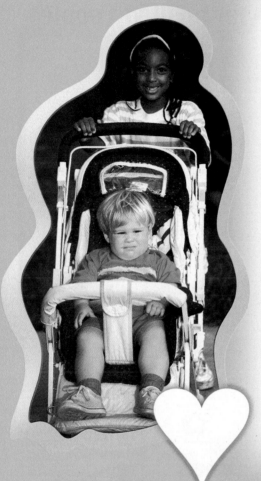

ACTIVITY *Color the ♡s in the photos of people showing kindness and respect.*

The Church Shares God's Love

The Church shares God's love as Jesus did. The Church cares for people as Jesus did. The Church treats people with kindness and respect.

The Church takes care of those who need help. The Church gives food to people who are hungry.

The Church gives a place to stay to people who have no place to live. The Church cares for people who are sick.

How can you show people kindness and respect?

Our Catholic Faith

Lord, Have Mercy

At Mass we pray, "Lord, have mercy." Mercy is another word for kindness. Jesus told us that people who are kind, or merciful, are blessed by God.

What Difference Does Faith Make in My Life?

Jesus shared God's love with people. You share God's love with others by your words and actions of kindness.

In the kite write or draw one way you are a sign of God's love.

I Am a Sign of God's Love

My Faith Choice

Choose one way to help others know God's love. This week I will do what I wrote or drew in the kite.

An Act of Love

We show we love Jesus when we treat people as he did. Learn to sign the prayer "Jesus, I love you." Pray the prayer together and by yourself.

Jesus,

I love you.

We Remember

Circle the word that best completes each sentence.

1. Jesus is the _____ of God.
   Son   Angel

2. _____ is the mother of Jesus.
   Anne   Mary

3. _____ is the foster father of Jesus.
   Joachim   Joseph

To Help You Remember

1. Jesus is the son of Mary and the Son of God.

2. The family of Jesus, Mary, and Joseph is the Holy Family.

3. Jesus shared God's love with everyone.

This Week . . .

In chapter 3, "Jesus Is the Son of God," your child learned that Jesus is the son of Mary and the Son of God. When it became time for God to send the promised Savior, he sent the angel Gabriel to the Blessed Virgin Mary. Gabriel announced to Mary that she would become the mother of the Savior, the Son of God who she was to name Jesus. Jesus is truly God and truly man. The Son of God became truly human without giving up being God. This mystery of faith is called the Incarnation. The family of Jesus, Mary, and Joseph is called the Holy Family. Jesus' life in the Holy Family prepared him for the work the Father sent him to do.

For more on the teachings of the Catholic Church on the mystery of the Incarnation of the Son of God and the public life of Jesus, see *Catechism of the Catholic Church* paragraph numbers 456–478 and 512–560.

Sharing God's Word

Read together the Bible story in Luke 2:1–20 about the shepherds who rushed to see the newborn Jesus or read the adaptation of the story on page 30. Emphasize that Jesus is truly God and truly man.

Praying

In this chapter your child signed an act of love. Learn and sign the prayer on page 35 together.

Making a Difference

Choose one of the following activities to do as a family or design a similar activity of your own.

- Talk together about the ways that each family member shows their love for God through their actions and words of respect and kindness.

- Choose to do an act that shows kindness and respect to people who are not members of your family. For example, as a family visit someone who is lonely or help an elderly neighbor.

- Make a poster with the heading "Jesus." Write all the things your family knows and believes about Jesus. For example, Jesus was born to Mary; Jesus is the Son of God; Jesus healed people; Jesus shared God's love with everyone.

For more ideas on ways your family can live your faith, visit the "Faith First for Families" page at **www.FaithFirst.com**. Share some of the ideas on this week's "Gospel Reflections" page.

Mary Is the Mother of God

A Scripture Story

We Pray

Hail Mary, full of grace, the Lord is with you.
                    Amen.

What is your favorite family story?

We listen to stories about people in our family. When we listen to the Bible, we learn stories about Mary.

What Bible stories do you know that tell us about Mary?

Angel Gabriel greeting Mary

37

Bible Background

Faith Focus

What does the Bible tell us about Mary?

Faith Words

Bible
The Bible is the written word of God. It is God's very own word to us.

angels
Angels give honor and glory to God. They are God's messengers and helpers.

The Bible Is God's Word to Us

God chose people to write stories about his love for us. We read these stories in the **Bible.** The Bible is God's very own word to us. It is a holy book because it is the written word of God.

When we listen to Bible stories, we learn about God and God's love. We learn about the people God chose to be his family. We read about Abraham and Sarah. We read about Mary and Joseph and many other people in God's family.

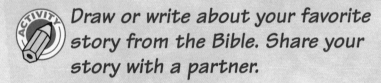 Draw or write about your favorite story from the Bible. Share your story with a partner.

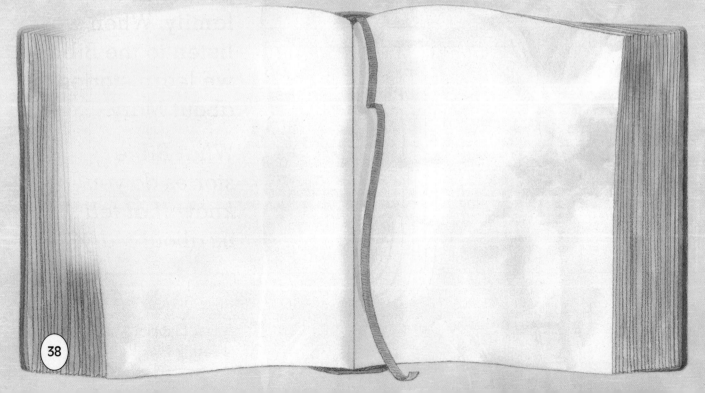

Mary Listens to God's Message

Angels are messengers of God. God sent the angel Gabriel to a young woman named Mary. The angel gave Mary this message from God. The angel said,

> "You are blessed, Mary. The Holy Spirit will come to you. You will have a baby. The baby's name will be Jesus. He will be the Son of God."

Mary listened carefully to the angel Gabriel. Then she said to Gabriel, "Yes, I will do what God wants me to do."

Based on Luke 1:28, 31, 35, 38

QUESTION *What did the angel tell Mary? What did Mary tell the angel?*

Mary Said Yes to God

Mary listened carefully to the angel and said yes to God. This showed that Mary had faith in God and trusted God. Mary loved God with her whole heart.

God asks us to have faith in him too. God asks us to trust him and to love him with our whole heart.

We have faith and trust in God. We have faith that God will always be with us. We trust that God always loves us. We show we love God when we say yes to God as Mary did.

ACTIVITY *Check (✔) ways you can say yes to God.*

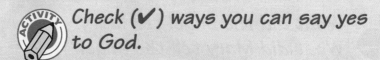

I Say Yes to God

___ Pray every day. ___ Share my toys.

___ Play fairly. ___ Act mean.

___ Help at home. ___ Say "Thank you."

The Church Honors Mary

Many Catholic churches are named after Mary. Here are some of the names of Catholic churches named after Mary.

Mary Immaculate

Nuestra Señora de los Dolores

Holy Rosary

Our Lady of Peace

Our Lady of Mount Carmel

Churches named after Mary help us to remember God's love for Mary. They help us to remember Mary's love for God. They help us to love God as Mary did.

QUESTION *What is one way you honor Mary and show her you love her?*

Our Catholic Faith

Feast Days

The Church honors and shows our love for Mary on special days each year. These are called feast days. Each year on January 1 we celebrate the feast of Mary, the Mother of God. This is a holy day of obligation. We have the responsibility to take part in the celebration of Mass.

Our Lady of Peace

Our Lady of Pe

What Difference Does Faith Make in My Life?

Mary showed her faith and love for God. You show your faith and love for God by what you say and do too.

Look at the activity on page 40. Choose one of the things you checked. Draw or write about it in this space.

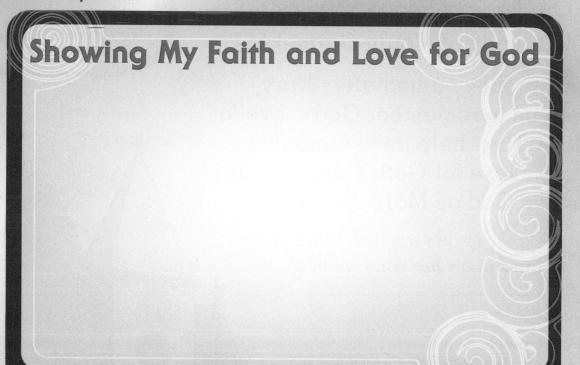

Showing My Faith and Love for God

My Faith Choice

This week I will show my faith and love for God. I will do what I have written about or have drawn above.

We Listen

Psalms are prayers in the Bible. We pray a Psalm after the first reading at Mass.

Leader: Mary listened to God's word.

All: **Happy are the people who listen to God's word.**

Based on Psalm 1:1–2

Leader: We listen to God's word.

All: **Happy are the people who listen to God's word.**

Leader: We say yes to God.

All: **Happy are the people who listen to God's word.**

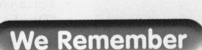

We Remember

Color the spaces with Xs one color and the spaces with Os other colors. Discover the name for the written word of God.

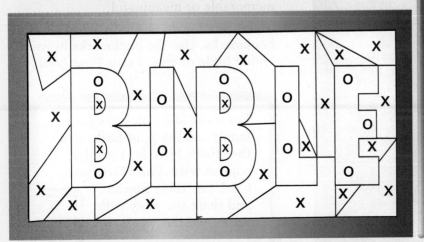

To Help You Remember

1. The Bible is God's very own word to us.

2. The Bible tells us about Mary's faith in God.

3. The Bible tells us about Mary's love for God.

This Week . . .

In chapter 4, "Mary Is the Mother of God: A Scripture Story," your child explored the Church's teaching that the Bible is the inspired, written word of God. God is the real author of the Bible. The Holy Spirit inspired the human writers of the Bible to assure that God's word would be faithfully and accurately communicated. Your child listened to and explored the Bible story of the Annunciation, which is told in Luke 1:26–38. The story shares with us Mary's faith and trust in God and her love for God. Faith includes a personal response to God who reveals himself.

For more on the teachings of the Catholic Church on the Bible and the Blessed Virgin Mary and her unique role in God's plan of goodness for the world, see *Catechism of the Catholic Church* paragraph numbers 101–133 and 484–507.

Sharing God's Word

Read together the Bible story in Luke 1:26–38 about the angel Gabriel announcing God's message to Mary or read the adaptation of the story on page 39. Emphasize Mary's faith and trust in God and her love for him.

Praying

In this chapter your child prayed a prayer using a psalm response. Read and pray together the prayer on page 43.

Making a Difference

Choose one of the following activities to do as a family or design a similar activity of your own.

- Teach your child the Mass responses "Thanks be to God" and "Praise to you, Lord Jesus Christ." Guide your child to use these responses properly when your family takes part in the celebration of Mass.

- Ask family members to share their favorite Scripture stories. Share what it is about each story that makes it so memorable or meaningful.

- Make "We Listen to God's Word" bookmarks. Use the bookmarks in your family Bible or your **Faith First** book.

For more ideas on ways your family can live your faith, visit the "Faith First for Families" page at **www.FaithFirst.com**. Click on "Bible Stories" and share the story with your child this week.

Jesus Shows God's Love

We Pray

God our Father, we thank you for your Son, Jesus Christ. Amen.

How do family members show love for one another?

We share our love for our family in many ways. Jesus shared God's love with people.

What are some ways Jesus shared God's love with people?

Jesus Loves Us

How did Jesus show his love for us?

cross

The cross is a sign of our faith in Jesus. It reminds us that Jesus died on a cross so that we could live forever in heaven.

disciples

Disciples are followers of Jesus.

Jesus Died on the Cross

Jesus always shared God's love with people. He helped people in many ways. He forgave the people who hurt him.

Some people did not want Jesus to teach and help others. They had Jesus killed on a **cross.** This is called the Crucifixion.

Because he loved us, Jesus died on a cross for all of us. He forgave the people who put him on the cross. He forgives us when we sin. Jesus died so that we could live with him forever in heaven.

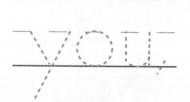 *Trace the words. Pray the prayer each day to thank Jesus for his love.*

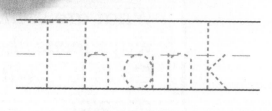

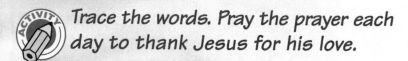 Thank you

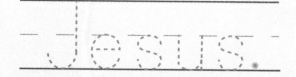 Jesus.

Jesus Is Alive

After Jesus died on the cross, his friends buried his body. Three days later some women who were **disciples,** or followers, of Jesus went to the place where Jesus was buried. The women were surprised at what they saw and heard. The Bible tells us,

> When the women came to the tomb, they saw men in white robes. "Jesus is not here," the men said. "He has been raised from the dead. Go and tell the other disciples of Jesus."
> Based on Luke 24:1–4, 6; Matthew 28:7

The women disciples of Jesus did what they were told. They went to the other disciples. They told them that Jesus was raised from the dead.

 Pretend you are with the women. What would you tell people?

Jesus Returned to His Father

After Jesus was raised from the dead, he stayed with his disciples for forty days. The Risen Jesus told his disciples to tell everyone in the world about him. Jesus told the disciples to invite everyone to believe in him and to be baptized.

Then Jesus returned to his Father in heaven. We call this the Ascension. After we die we too will return to God the Father in heaven.

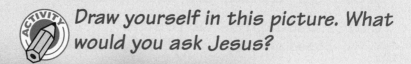 *Draw yourself in this picture. What would you ask Jesus?*

We Remember Jesus

We see many candles in our church. The tallest lighted candle is called the Easter candle. It reminds us that Jesus has been raised from the dead.

The Church uses lighted candles to help us to remember that Jesus brings light to the world. At Baptism we receive a candle that is lighted from the Easter candle. This reminds us that we are to live our faith in Jesus. We are to be lights in the world. We are to tell people about Jesus. We are to tell people the good news that God loves them.

QUESTION *Who are some of the people who tell you about Jesus?*

Our Catholic Faith

Candlemas Day

Each year the Church blesses candles on February 2. This day is called Candlemas Day. We use these candles in our churches and in our homes. They remind us of Jesus, the Light of the world. We are to be lights in the world.

What Difference Does Faith Make in My Life?

When you tell others about Jesus, you are sharing God's love with people. You are a light in the world.

Make a poster that tells people about Jesus. Use your poster as a reminder to act as a follower of Jesus.

JESUS

My Faith Choice

This week I will share my poster. I will tell someone about Jesus.

We Pray

A Litany to Jesus

A litany is a prayer. One part of a litany is repeated over and over. Pray this litany with your class.

Leader: Jesus, Son of God, by your death,

All: **you show us God's love.**

Leader: Jesus, Son of God, by your Resurrection,

All: **you show us God's love.**

Leader: Jesus, Son of God, by your return to your Father,

All: **you show us God's love.**

We Remember

Draw lines from the words in Column A to the sentences they complete in Column B.

Column A	Column B
1. **forgives**	a. God ___ Jesus from the dead.
2. **raised**	b. Jesus died on a ___ for all of us.
3. **cross**	c. Jesus ___ us when we sin.

To Help You Remember

1. Jesus loved us so much that he gave his life for us.

2. God raised Jesus from the dead.

3. Jesus returned to his Father in heaven.

This Week . . .

In chapter 5, "Jesus Shows God's Love," your child discovered that Jesus showed his great love for us by dying on the cross. Three days after his death, Jesus was raised from the dead. Forty days later, Jesus ascended, or returned, to his Father in heaven. Before he ascended to heaven, Jesus commanded the disciples to evangelize the world. This means they were to tell all people about him and his teaching. They were to make disciples of all people and to baptize them.

For more on the teachings of the Catholic Church on the mystery of Jesus' suffering, death, Resurrection, and Ascension, see *Catechism of the Catholic Church* paragraph numbers 561, 620–621, 629, 656–665.

Sharing God's Word

Read together the Bible story in Luke 24:1–12 about the Resurrection or read the adaptation of the story on page 47. Emphasize that as the first disciples did, we are to tell people about Jesus.

Praying

In this chapter your child prayed a litany. Read and pray together the prayer on page 51.

Making a Difference

Choose one of the following activities to do as a family or design a similar activity of your own.

• Jesus told the disciples to tell everyone about him. This week your family can follow Jesus' command and tell others about him. Invite someone you know to take part in an activity at church with your family.

• Jesus tells us that we are to be lights in the world. Each night at dinner, light a candle as part of your mealtime prayer. Take turns telling about how each family member was a light in the world that day.

• It is difficult to know everyone in your parish. Each month make an effort to introduce yourselves as a family to one new family in your parish.

For more ideas on ways your family can live your faith, visit the "Faith First for Families" page at **www.FaithFirst.com**. The "Make a Difference" page goes especially well with this chapter.

The Good Samaritan

A Scripture Story

The good Samaritan helping the injured man

We Pray

Lord God, help us to love others as you love them.
Amen.

What stories do you know that help you to make good choices?

Jesus sometimes told stories to teach us how to live as his disciples.

What story of Jesus have you heard that teaches you to live as a follower of Jesus?

Bible Background

Faith Focus

What does the story of the Good Samaritan teach us?

Faith Words

Old Testament
The Old Testament is the first main part of the Bible.

New Testament
The New Testament is the second main part of the Bible.

The Bible

The Bible has many stories that Jesus told. When we listen to Bible stories, we believe God is telling us about himself and his love for us.

The Bible has two main parts. The first part of the Bible is the **Old Testament.** The Old Testament was written before Jesus was born.

The second part of the Bible is the **New Testament.** It tells us about Jesus. The New Testament was written after Jesus died and returned to heaven.

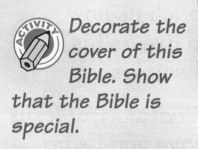 Decorate the cover of this Bible. Show that the Bible is special.

Bible

54

The Good Samaritan

The stories Jesus told are in the Gospels. The Gospels are in the New Testament. Here is one story Jesus told. He said,

One day robbers attacked a man on a road. They hurt the man and left him lying on the road.

A traveler from Samaria saw the injured man. He stopped and put bandages on the man's wounds. The Samaritan brought the injured man to an inn. He told the innkeeper, "Take care of this man. I will pay you whatever it costs."

Based on Luke 10:30, 33–35

QUESTION

Why do you think Jesus told the story of the Good Samaritan?

①

②

③

A Good Neighbor

The story of the Good Samaritan helps us to live as followers of Jesus. It teaches that God wants us to help one another. God wants us to help people even when we do not feel like helping. This story teaches us to be good neighbors to one another.

ACTIVITY *Finish the picture story. Draw or write about how the children can act as good Samaritans.*

Catholic Hospitals

The Catholic Church is a good neighbor to all people. We take care of people who are sick. This is one way the Church is a good neighbor.

Catholics build hospitals to care for the sick. There are Catholic hospitals all over the world. Sometimes these hospitals are named Good Samaritan Hospital.

QUESTION Who are the people who care for you when you are sick? How can you be a good neighbor when a friend is sick?

Our Catholic Faith

Prayer of the Faithful

We are good neighbors when we pray for one another. Each Sunday at Mass we pray the Prayer of the Faithful. In this prayer we pray for people who are sick.

What Difference Does Faith Make in My Life?

You can be a good Samaritan. You can be a good neighbor. You can show people how much God loves them and cares about them.

Color a ☺ next to ways you can help someone this week as Jesus taught. Then write one other way you can help.

Living as a Good Samaritan

☺ Say kind words to someone who is sad.

☺ Help fold laundry at home.

☺ Give a get-well card to someone who is sick.

☺ _____

_____ .

My Faith Choice

I will help someone this week. I will do one of the things in the above activity.

Prayer of the Faithful

We pray the Prayer of the Faithful at Mass.
We pray for other people.

Leader: Let us ask God to help us show our love for people.
For the pope and all the people of the Church,

All: **Lord, hear our prayer.**

Leader: For the leaders and people of our country,

All: **Lord, hear our prayer.**

Leader: Think of the people you wish to pray for (*pause*).

All: **Lord, hear our prayer.**

We Remember

Read each sentence. Circle Yes if the sentence is true. Circle No if it is not true.

1. The Bible has three main parts.
   Yes   **No**

2. The good Samaritan took care of the injured man.
   Yes   **No**

3. Jesus told stories to teach us to help others.
   Yes   **No**

To Help You Remember

1. Jesus told the story of the Good Samaritan to help us to live as his followers.

2. The Good Samaritan story teaches us that God wants us to care for one another.

3. The Good Samaritan story teaches us that God wants us to live as good neighbors.

This Week . . .

In chapter 6, "The Good Samaritan: A Scripture Story," your child learned about the Bible. The two main parts of the Bible are the forty-six books of the Old Testament and the twenty-seven books of the New Testament. The Gospel is at the center of the whole Bible because God has revealed himself most fully in his Son, Jesus Christ. The stories in the Bible help us come to know, love, and serve God. The Gospel story, or parable, of the Good Samaritan teaches us how we are to live as disciples of Jesus. We are to care about one another and to show our love by our actions as Jesus did.

For more on the teachings of the Catholic Church on Sacred Scripture and its importance for our life as followers of Jesus, see *Catechism of the Catholic Church* paragraph numbers 101–133.

Sharing God's Word

Read together the parable of the Good Samaritan in Luke 10:29–37 or you can read the adaptation of the parable on page 55. Emphasize that the Samaritan was a good neighbor because he stopped, took the time, and helped the injured man.

Praying

In this chapter your child prayed a prayer of the faithful, which is a prayer of intercession. Read and pray together the prayer on page 59.

Making a Difference

Choose one of the following activities to do as a family or design a similar activity of your own.

• This week when you take part in the celebration of Mass, help your child participate in the praying of the Prayer of the Faithful. After Mass, talk about the petitions that were used in the prayer. Include a prayer of the faithful in your family mealtime prayers this week.

• Talk about how your family can be good Samaritans to one another this week. For example, help one another out without having to be asked.

• Share with one another Gospel stories in which Jesus teaches you how God wants you to treat others. Emphasize how these stories guide you to live as a Christian family.

> For more ideas on ways your family can live your faith, visit the "Faith First for Families" page at **www.FaithFirst.com**. You will find the "Contemporary Issues" page helpful this week.

The Holy Spirit Is Our Helper

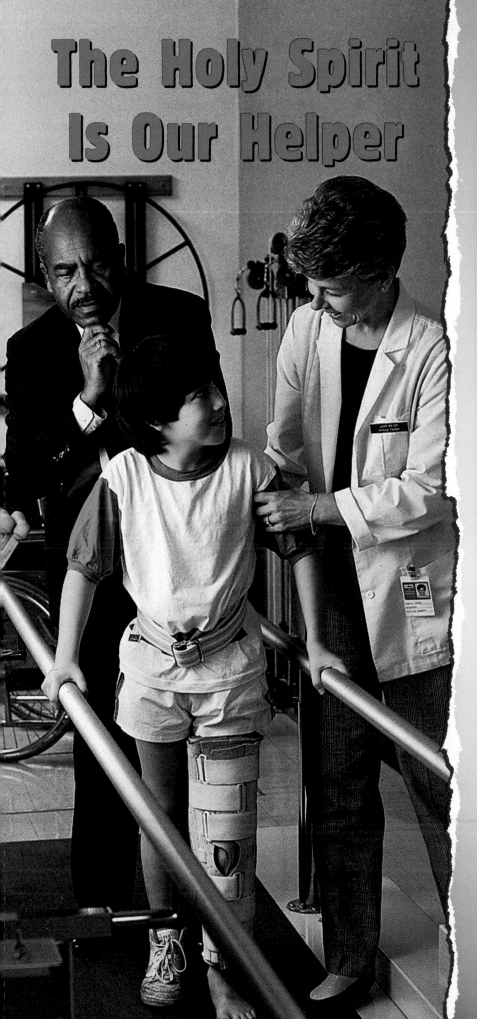

We Pray

Holy Spirit, fill our hearts with your love. Amen.

Who are some of the people who teach and help you to learn new things?

Everyone needs teachers and helpers. The Holy Spirit is our teacher and helper.

What do you know about the Holy Spirit?

Faith Focus

How does the Holy Spirit help us?

Faith Words

Holy Trinity
The Holy Trinity is one God in three Persons—God the Father, God the Son, and God the Holy Spirit.

Holy Spirit
The Holy Spirit is the third Person of the Holy Trinity. The Holy Spirit is always with us to be our helper.

The Holy Trinity

Jesus taught us that there is only one God. Jesus is the Son of God. He taught us about God the Father and God the Holy Spirit.

Jesus taught us that there is one God in three Persons. He taught us there is one God who is God the Father, God the Son, and God the Holy Spirit. The **Holy Trinity** is one God in three Persons.

 Pray the Sign of the Cross. This shows you believe in the Holy Trinity.

Father

Son

God

Holy Spirit

Jesus' Promise to Us

Jesus made a promise to his friends. He promised that God the Father would send them a helper. Jesus said,

> "The Father will give you a helper who will always be with you." Based on John 14:16

God the **Holy Spirit** is the helper that the Father would send. Jesus told his friends that the Holy Spirit would be their teacher and helper. The Holy Spirit would teach and help them to understand what Jesus said and did. The Holy Spirit would teach and help them to live as Jesus' followers.

ACTIVITY Color the spaces with Xs one color and the spaces with Os other colors. Find out the name of the third Person of the Holy Trinity.

The Holy Spirit Is with Us

The Holy Spirit is the third Person of the Holy Trinity. We first receive the gift of the Holy Spirit at Baptism. The Holy Spirit is always with us.

The Holy Spirit helps us to pray. The Holy Spirit helps us to learn what Jesus taught. Jesus told his followers,

"Love one another as I love you." Based on John 13:34

The Holy Spirit helps us to do what Jesus asked us to do. The Holy Spirit helps us to love God and one another.

ACTIVITY *In each box write the number of the picture that matches each of the sentences.*

☐ *I help my community.*

☐ *I help my family.*

☐ *I say my prayers.*

Our Church Makes a Difference

Signs of the Holy Spirit

We learn about God in many different ways. Some churches have stained-glass windows of Jesus, Mary, and the saints. Sometimes these colorful windows have symbols of the Holy Spirit. Flames of fire and a white dove are two symbols of the Holy Spirit.

The light shining through stained-glass windows reminds us of God's love for us. The love of God fills our hearts. The Holy Spirit helps us to share that love with others.

QUESTION *What are some symbols for the Holy Spirit that you see in your church?*

Our Catholic Faith

Signs and Symbols

Signs and symbols help us to understand the meaning of what God has told us. The Church uses a beautiful white dove as a sign of the Holy Spirit.

What Difference Does Faith Make in My Life?

God the Holy Spirit is always with you. The Holy Spirit is your helper and teacher.

Ask the Holy Spirit to help you show your love for someone as Jesus taught. Draw or write about what you will do.

The Holy Spirit Teaches Me to Love

My Faith Choice

This week I will remember that the Holy Spirit is with me. I will do what I drew or wrote about.

Prayer to the Holy Spirit

Learn this prayer to the Holy Spirit.
Pray it together, using gestures.

Come,

Holy Spirit,

fill our hearts with

the fire of

your love.

Amen.

We Remember

Circle the names in the puzzle. Share what each name tells about God.

> **Father**   **Son**   **Holy Spirit**

```
Q F A T H E R
W S O N E O P
H O L Y C M S
L S P I R I T
```

To Help You Remember

1. The Holy Spirit helps and teaches us to pray.

2. The Holy Spirit helps us to know what Jesus taught.

3. The Holy Spirit helps and teaches us to do what Jesus asked us to do.

With My Family

This Week . . .

In chapter 7, "The Holy Spirit Is Our Helper," your child learned about the Holy Spirit, the third Person of the Holy Trinity. The Holy Trinity is the mystery of one God in three divine Persons. Before Jesus died, he promised the disciples that he would not leave them alone. The Father would send them the Advocate. The Holy Spirit came to the disciples on Pentecost. The Holy Spirit is the Advocate that the Father sent and who is always with us. The Holy Spirit helps us to know and believe what Jesus revealed and to live as Jesus taught.

For more on the teachings of the Catholic Church on the mystery of the Holy Trinity and the Holy Spirit, see *Catechism of the Catholic Church* paragraph numbers 232–248 and 683–741.

Sharing God's Word

Read together the Gospel story in John 14:15–19 or the adaptation of the story on page 63. Emphasize that the Holy Spirit, the Advocate, is always with us to teach and help us live as Jesus taught.

Praying

In this chapter your child learned a prayer to the Holy Spirit. Read and pray together the prayer on page 67.

Making a Difference

Choose one of the following activities to do as a family or design a similar activity of your own.

- Make prayer cards, using the Prayer to the Holy Spirit on page 67. Decorate the cards with signs and symbols of the Holy Spirit. Keep the cards where they will serve as reminders that the Holy Spirit is always with your family as your teacher and helper.

- This week your child learned about the Holy Trinity. Now is a good time to review the Sign of the Cross with your child. Talk about how the Sign of the Cross names all three Persons of the Holy Trinity.

- At mealtimes this week pray to the Holy Spirit. Ask the Holy Spirit to help you live as a Christian family.

For more ideas on ways your family can live your faith, visit the "Faith First for Families" page at **www.FaithFirst.com**. Click on "Family Prayer" and pray the prayer of the week.

Jesus Gave Us the Church

We Pray

God our Father, we praise you. We are your people. Amen.

What do you and your family do that shows you are a family?

Each of us belongs to our family. We belong to the family of our Church.

How can people tell that you belong to the Church?

Faith Focus

Who helps us to live as followers of Jesus?

Faith Words

Church
The Church is the People of God who believe in Jesus and live as his followers.

Catholic
A Catholic is a follower of Jesus who is a member of the Catholic Church.

Who are the people in your church who help you to live as a follower of Jesus?

The People of God

The **Church** is the People of God. The Holy Spirit helps the Church to live as followers of Jesus.

On Pentecost the Holy Spirit came to the disciples as Jesus promised. Read what happened.

The disciples of Jesus were all together in a room. They heard a sound like a strong wind. Small flames settled over each person's head. The power of the Holy Spirit filled the disciples of Jesus.

Based on Acts of the Apostles 2:1–4

On Pentecost the disciples began the work Jesus told them to do. They told people about Jesus. They invited people to be baptized. The work of the Church began.

The Catholic Church

We belong to the Catholic Church. We become members of the Church at Baptism.

Catholics believe in Jesus Christ. Together we follow Jesus. We do what Jesus taught us. We learn about God and his love for us. We teach others about Jesus. We pray together. We share our love for Jesus with one another.

Use the code to find out four things Catholics do.

A	B	C	D	E	F	G	H	I	J	K	L	M
1	2	3	4	5	6	7	8	9	10	11	12	13

N	O	P	Q	R	S	T	U	V	W	X	Y	Z
14	15	16	17	18	19	20	21	22	23	24	25	26

12 5 1 18 14

16 18 1 25

8 5 12 16

20 5 1 3 8

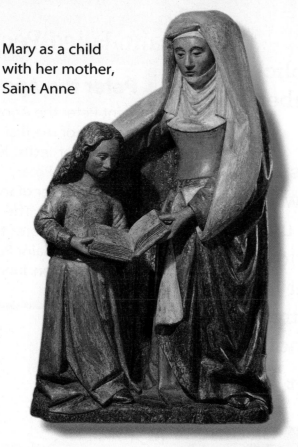

Mary as a child with her mother, Saint Anne

The Saints

Members of our Church family show us how to live as followers of Jesus. Some of these people are called saints. Saints are grown-ups and children from all races and from all over the world.

There are many saints named by the Church. These saints now live with Jesus in heaven. Mary, the mother of Jesus, is the greatest saint. We pray to Mary and the other saints. All the saints want to help us to live as children of God. They want us to be happy with God on earth and in heaven.

Draw a picture of someone showing you how to live as a child of God.

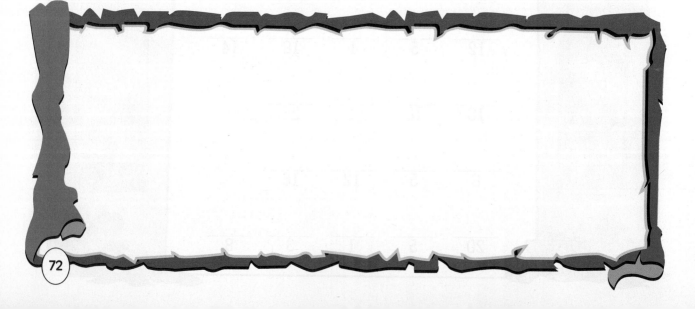

Our Church Makes a Difference

Our Church Community

The Church is a community. The Church is the People of God who believe in Jesus and live as his followers.

Our Catholic Faith

The Pope

The pope is the pastor of the whole Catholic Church. The pope helps us to live as followers of Jesus.

All the members of the Church, grown-ups and children, work together. We tell people all over the world about Jesus Christ. The Holy Spirit works with the Church to make people followers of Jesus.

Who are some of the members of your church family? How do they teach you and other people about Jesus?

What Difference Does Faith Make in My Life?

You belong to the Church. The saints and other members of the Church help you to live as a follower of Jesus.

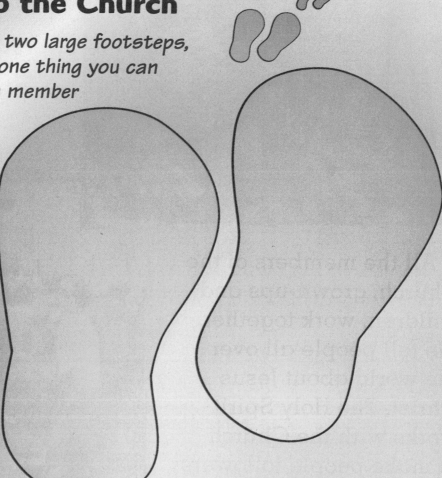

I Belong to the Church

In each of the two large footsteps, write or draw one thing you can do to live as a member of the Church.

My Faith Choice

I can show that I am a member of the Catholic Church. This week I will do what I wrote or drew above.

We Pray

Litany of the Saints

The Church prays the Litany to the Saints. Pray this part of the Litany of the Saints together.

Leader: Holy Mary, Mother of God
All: **pray for us.**

Leader: Saint Joseph
All: **pray for us.**

Leader: Saint Anne
All: **pray for us.**

Leader: Saint Peter
All: **pray for us.**

Leader: All holy men and women
All: **pray for us.**

We Remember

Complete the sentences. Color the circle next to the best choice.

1. The __ came to Jesus' followers on Pentecost.
   ○ Holy Trinity   ○ Holy Spirit

2. __ is the greatest saint.
   ○ Peter   ○ Mary

3. Peter told the people about __.
   ○ Jesus   ○ Mary

To Help You Remember

1. The Holy Spirit helps all the members of the Church.

2. The Church helps us to do what Jesus taught us.

3. The saints of the Church help us to live as followers of Jesus.

Grade 1 • Chapter 8   75

This Week . . .

In chapter 8, "Jesus Gave Us the Church," your child discovered that the Church began on Pentecost. On Pentecost the Holy Spirit came upon the disciples, and they received the power to go out and preach to others about Jesus. God has called us together in Christ to be the new People of God. Christ is the Head of the Church, the Body of Christ. We are members of the Catholic Church. We believe in Jesus Christ and in everything he revealed to us. We work together as the Body of Christ to share our love for Jesus with others. The saints provide us with examples of how to live as disciples of Jesus Christ in the world today.

For more on the teachings of the Catholic Church on the mystery of the Church, see *Catechism of the Catholic Church* paragraph numbers 737–741 and 748–801.

Sharing God's Word

Read together the Bible story in Acts 2:1–41 about Pentecost or read the adaptation of the story on page 70. Emphasize that on Pentecost the Holy Spirit came to the disciples, and the disciples began the work of the Church.

Praying

In this chapter your child prayed part of the Litany of the Saints. Read and pray together the prayer on page 75.

Making a Difference

Choose one of the following activities to do as a family or design a similar activity of your own.

- Identify and name ways you live as members of the Catholic Church. For example, we take part in Mass, we help the poor and hungry, we pray and learn about Jesus and all he revealed.

- The saints show us how to live as followers of Jesus. If your parish is named after a saint, take time this week to find out more about the saint. Talk about how this saint or another saint, if your parish is not named after a saint, helps you live as a Christian family.

- The Church helps us live as followers of Jesus. Talk about the many ways your parish helps your family live as followers of Jesus.

For more ideas on ways your family can live your faith, visit the "Faith First for Families" page at **www.FaithFirst.com**. You are only a click away from taking a "Tour of a Church" with your child this week.

The First Christians Follow Jesus

A Scripture Story

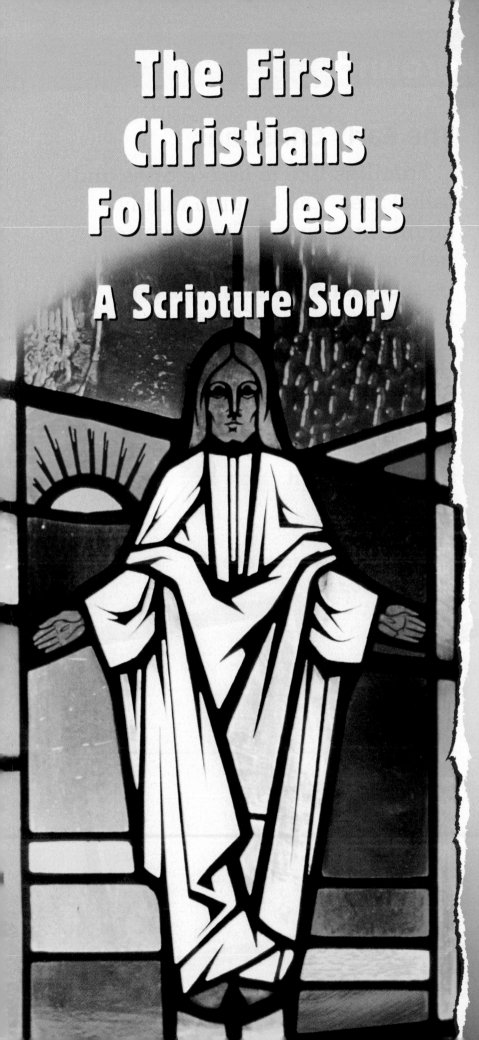

We Pray

God, thank you for gathering us around Jesus as one family.
Amen.

What are some things your family does together?

Families do many things together. Christian families show by their actions and words that they are followers of Jesus.

What does your Church family do that shows you are followers of Jesus?

Bible Background

Faith Focus

How did the early Christians live?

Faith Words

Christians
Christians are followers of Jesus Christ. They believe in Jesus Christ and live as he taught.

The Early Christians

Families like to hear stories and tell stories. Our Church family shares stories too. These stories help us to know what it means to be a Christian. **Christians** are followers of Jesus Christ.

Our Church shares stories about what Christians did a long time ago. We can read many stories about the first Christians in the New Testament.

Following Jesus

On each of the road signs write or draw one thing followers of Jesus do today.

The First Christians

This is a story from the New Testament. It tells how the first Christians lived.

The first Christians spent time learning what Jesus taught. They shared their money and belongings with one another. They prayed together. They broke and shared bread together. Together they praised God.

Many people saw how the first Christians treated one another with kindness and love. Soon many other people became followers of Jesus.

Based on Acts of the Apostles 2:42, 45–47

We are Christians. We do the same things the first Christians did.

What is something that the first Christians did that Christians also do today?

Read each sentence about the early Christians. Check (✔) each thing that Christians also do today.

We Love God and Others

Jesus taught us how to live as children of God. He taught us to love God and to love our neighbors.

The first Christians showed their love for God. They prayed. They shared the Eucharist. They thanked God for everything.

The first Christians showed their love for one another. They shared what they had with each other. They helped people in need.

Early Christians	Christians Today
Prayed together.	☐
Cared for one another.	☐
Learned about Jesus.	☐
Shared what they had with others.	☐

Saint Martin de Porres

Saint Martin de Porres loved God and other people as Jesus taught us to do. Martin became a religious brother. He worked with poor people whom nobody else was helping.

Brother Martin opened a home for children whose parents died or could not care for them. He opened a hospital and schools. He also took care of animals that were sick or hungry.

The Church has named Brother Martin a saint. Today many people follow the example of Saint Martin de Porres. Martin de Porres House of Hospitality serves breakfast and lunch to hundreds of people six days a week.

 Who is someone you know who helps people as Saint Martin de Porres did?

Our Catholic Faith

Patron Saints

The Church names some saints to be patron saints. Saint Martin de Porres is the patron saint of African-Americans and community health workers. Patron saints are saints a person or group of people ask to help them to live as followers of Jesus.

MARTIN DE PORRES

What Difference Does Faith Make in My Life?

Christians today love God and others as the first Christians did. Each day you try your best to live as Jesus taught.

Draw a ☺ next to each thing that you can do this week to live as Jesus taught.

Living as a Christian

○ Say my prayers.

○ Hurt someone.

○ Learn about Jesus.

○ Share my toys.

○ Play fairly.

○ Speak unkind words.

○ Help at home.

○ Pay attention at school.

My Faith Choice

This week I will try to do what the first Christians did. I will do what I have checked.

We Pray

Sign of Peace

We are invited to share a sign of peace at Mass. This shows we want to live as Jesus taught.

Leader: We thank you, God, for the Church.

All: **Praise the Lord, for he is good!**

Leader: Let us share a sign of peace with one another.

All: Share a handshake or other sign of peace and friendship.

We Remember

Read each sentence. Circle Yes if the sentence is true. Circle No if it is not true.

1. The first Christians shared stories about Jesus. **Yes   No**

2. The first Christians prayed together. **Yes   No**

3. The first Christians shared their belongings with one another. **Yes   No**

To Help You Remember

1. Christians are people who believe in and follow Jesus Christ.

2. The first Christians gathered together and showed how much they loved God and one another.

3. Christians today show their love for one another just as the first Christians did.

This Week . . .

In chapter 9, "The First Christians Follow Jesus: A Scripture Story," your child learned that the first Christians gathered to express their faith and belief in Jesus. They listened to the teachings of the Apostles. They shared all they had with one another, especially with people in need. They gathered to pray and break bread, or share the Eucharist. Christians today do the same things that the first Christians did. Every member of the Church is called to cooperate with the grace of the Holy Spirit and work together to live as Jesus taught.

For more on the teachings of the Catholic Church on the mystery of the Church and its work in the world, see *Catechism of the Catholic Church* paragraph numbers 849–852, 1397, and 2030–2046.

Sharing God's Word

Read together the Bible story in Acts 2:42–47 about the first Christians or read the adaptation of the story on page 79. Emphasize that the first Christians shared their possessions with people in need and were known for their love for one another.

Praying

In this chapter your child prayed using a sign of peace. Read and pray together the prayer on page 83.

Making a Difference

Choose one of the following activities to do as a family or design a similar activity of your own.

- Identify ways that your family lives as the first Christians did. Talk about ways you pray together, learn about Jesus together, and share things as a family. Invite each family member to choose one thing they can do to help your family live as a Christian family.

- Decide one way your family can share your time and possessions with other people in your parish or neighborhood. For example, donate food or clothing to those in need. Take the time to do it.

- Make a banner out of paper or cloth that says "They will know we are Christians by our love." Hang it for all family members to see.

For more ideas on ways your family can live your faith, visit the "Faith First for Families" page at **www.FaithFirst.com**. The "Make a Difference" page goes especially well with this chapter.

Review Unit 1

Name _____

A. The Best Word or Phrase

Complete the sentences. Color the circle next to the best choice.

1. Faith is a gift from God that helps us to know God and to ___ in him.

   ○ hope   ○ believe

2. Jesus treated ___ people with respect.

   ○ all   ○ some

3. The Bible is ___ very own word to us.

   ○ the Church's   ○ God's

4. The ___ came to Jesus' disciples on Pentecost as Jesus promised.

   ○ Holy Spirit   ○ saints

5. The ___ is one God in three Persons.

   ○ Holy Family   ○ Holy Trinity

B. Words About Jesus

Circle the numbers next to the words that tell about Jesus.

1. Son of God   4. died on the cross

2. Holy Spirit   5. told stories to teach us

3. Loving Father   6. was raised from the dead

C. What I Learned

1. What new thing have you learned about Jesus? Tell a partner.

2. Look at the "Words to Know" on page 12. Circle the words that you know now.

D. From a Scripture Story

Draw two pictures about the story that Jesus told about the good Samaritan. Tell something from the beginning and end of the story.

Beginning	End

Unit 2 • We Worship

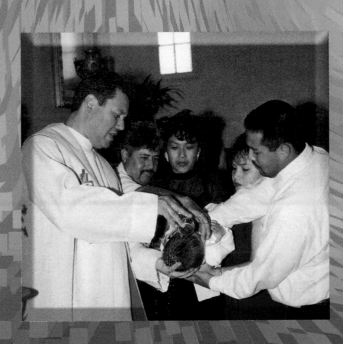

What are some ways we worship God as Catholics?

Getting Ready

What I Have Learned

What is something you already know about these faith words?

Lent

_____

_____

Baptism

_____

_____

The Mass

_____

_____

Words to Know

Put an X next to the faith words you know. Put a ? next to the faith words you need to know more about.

Faith Words

_____ Church year

_____ Easter

_____ sacraments

_____ Gospel

_____ Eucharist

_____ miracle

A Question I Have

What question would you like to ask about the Mass?

_____

_____

_____

_____

From a Scripture Story

Jesus feeding the crowd

What foods did Jesus use to feed the crowd?

The Church Celebrates All Year

We Pray

God our Father, you always show your love for us.   Amen.

What is your favorite season of the year?

Winter, spring, summer, and fall are the seasons of the year. The Church's year has seasons too.

What are the names of the seasons of the Church's year?

Faith Focus

What is the Church's year?

Faith Words

Church's year
The Church's year is made up of five seasons. They are Advent, Christmas, Lent, Easter, and Ordinary Time.

Easter
Easter is the season of the Church's year when we celebrate that Jesus was raised from the dead.

ACTIVITY Color three candles purple and one candle pink in the Advent wreath. Tell how your parish or your family uses an Advent wreath to celebrate Advent.

The Seasons of the Church

The different times of the **Church's year** are called its seasons. Advent, Christmas, Lent, Easter, and Ordinary Time are the seasons of the Church's year.

Each season of the Church's year tells us something about Jesus. All year long we remember God's love for us.

Advent

Advent is the first season of the Church's year. The Advent wreath reminds us to prepare for Christmas. We get our hearts ready for Jesus. The color for Advent is purple.

Christmas

Christmas comes after Advent. During the Christmas season we remember the birth of Jesus. Jesus is God's greatest gift to us. He is God's Son who came to live on earth with us.

The Church's celebration of Christmas is not just one day. The season of Christmas lasts about two or three weeks. We use the color white to celebrate Christmas.

Joseph

Saint Joseph was the husband of Mary and the foster father of Jesus. The angel told Joseph that Mary was going to have a baby. The angel also told Joseph to give the baby the name Jesus. The Church celebrates the feast day of Saint Joseph on March 19.

ACTIVITY

Look at the picture. Tell the Christmas story to a classmate. Ask a classmate to tell you the Christmas story.

Lent

During Lent we remember that Jesus died for us on the cross. We get ready for Easter. We try harder to be kind and loving. The color for Lent is purple.

Easter

Easter celebrates that Jesus was raised from the dead. This is the most important celebration of the whole Church year. We see the lighted Easter candle in our church. It reminds us that Jesus was raised from the dead. The color for Easter is white.

Ordinary Time

During Ordinary Time we listen to Bible stories about what Jesus said and did. We learn to be followers of Jesus. The color for Ordinary Time is green.

Color the symbols for Lent and Easter and Ordinary Time. Share with a partner what each symbol reminds us of Jesus.

Celebrating Sunday

Sunday is the Lord's Day. We keep Sunday holy. Every Sunday we gather together for Mass. On every Sunday we remember that Jesus was raised from the dead.

Sunday is a special family day too. We spend time together. We celebrate that our family is part of God's family.

QUESTION *How does your family celebrate Sunday, the Lord's Day?*

Our Catholic Faith

Holy Days of Obligation

In addition to Sunday, Catholics have the responsibility to take part in Mass on other days. These days are called holy days of obligation.

What Difference Does Faith Make in My Life?

You remember all that Jesus did for us when you celebrate the seasons of the Church's year. You celebrate God's love with other people in your Church family.

Celebrating God's Love

In the small candle write the name of one of the seasons of the Church's year. In the large candle write or draw how you celebrate that season.

My Faith Choice

I will celebrate the season of the Church's year we are celebrating right now. I will

_____

_____.

We Pray

Lord, We Praise You

Each day the Church praises God for his goodness and love. Pray this prayer of praise together.

Group 1: In the morning and the night,
All: Lord, we praise you.

Group 2: In the summer and the fall,
All: Lord, we praise you.

Group 1: In the winter and the spring,
All: Lord, we praise you.

Group 2: Every day of the year,
All: All people praise you, Lord.

We Remember

Draw lines to match the Church seasons with what we celebrate.

Easter

Christmas

Lent

Advent

● We get ready for Easter.

● We celebrate that Jesus was raised from the dead.

● We get ready for Christmas.

● We remember the birth of Jesus.

To Help You Remember

1. The Church has special times, or seasons, of the year.

2. The Church's year is made up of Advent, Christmas, Lent, Easter, and Ordinary Time.

3. Sunday is the Lord's Day.

This Week . . .

In chapter 10, "The Church Celebrates All Year," your child learned that the Church's year has special seasons just as the calendar year has. The seasons of the Church's year are Advent, Christmas, Lent, Easter, and Ordinary Time. The Easter Triduum of Holy Thursday, Good Friday, and the Easter Vigil/Easter Sunday are the heart and center of the Church's liturgical year. During the Church's year we celebrate and share in the Paschal Mystery of Christ's Passion, death, Resurrection, and Ascension. We join with Christ all year long and share in his work of salvation.

For more on the teachings of the Catholic Church on the Church's year, see *Catechism of the Catholic Church* paragraph numbers 1163–1173.

Sharing God's Word

Read together Psalm 150. Emphasize that all throughout the liturgical year the Church gives praise and thanksgiving to God.

Praying

In this chapter your child prayed a prayer of praise. Read and pray together the prayer on page 95.

Making a Difference

Choose one of the following activities to do as a family or design a similar activity of your own.

- When you take part in Mass this week, look around and listen for all the signs that tell you what season of the Church year the Church is now celebrating.

- Choose an activity that will help you celebrate the current liturgical season. For example, during Advent you can use an Advent calendar to help anticipate and prepare for Christmas.

- Make a banner to hang in your home that will remind you of the current season of the Church's year. Look for ways to celebrate that season at home as a family. For example, during Lent take part in Operation Rice Bowl.

For more ideas on ways your family can live your faith, visit the "Faith First for Families" page at **www.FaithFirst.com**. You will find it helpful to take a look at "Questions Kids Ask."

The Church's Celebrations

We Pray

God our loving Father, may I walk always as a child of the light. Amen.

What special days does your family celebrate?

Families celebrate birthdays and other special times. Baptism is one of the special celebrations of the Church.

What do you know about your Baptism?

Faith Focus

What do we celebrate at Baptism and Confirmation?

Faith Words

sacraments
The sacraments are the seven signs and celebrations of God's love that Jesus gave the Church.

Baptism
Baptism is the first sacrament we celebrate. In Baptism we receive the gift of God's life and become members of the Church.

God Shares His Love

Jesus gave the Church seven special signs and celebrations of God's love. We call these celebrations the **sacraments.**

The sacraments celebrate that God is with us. These are the names of the seven sacraments.

Baptism

Confirmation

Eucharist

Penance and Reconciliation

Anointing of the Sick

Holy Orders

Matrimony

In the sacraments God shares his love and life with us. Each of the seven sacraments helps us to grow closer to God.

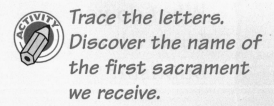
Trace the letters. Discover the name of the first sacrament we receive.

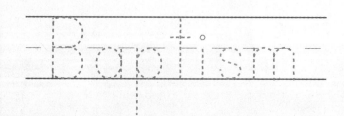

We Celebrate Baptism

Baptism is the first sacrament we celebrate. We become a member of the Church. The priest or deacon pours water on our head or puts us in the water three times. As he does this, he says, "I baptize you in the name of the Father, and of the Son, and of the Holy Spirit. Amen."

This shows we receive the gift of God's life. We receive the gift of the Holy Spirit. Original sin and any other sins we have committed are forgiven. Original sin is the first sin committed by Adam and Eve. Everyone is born with this sin.

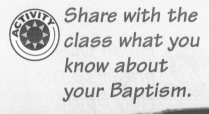

Faith-Filled People

Godparents

Godparents help us to grow in faith. They show us how to love God and other people as Jesus taught.

Share with the class what you know about your Baptism.

ACTIVITY

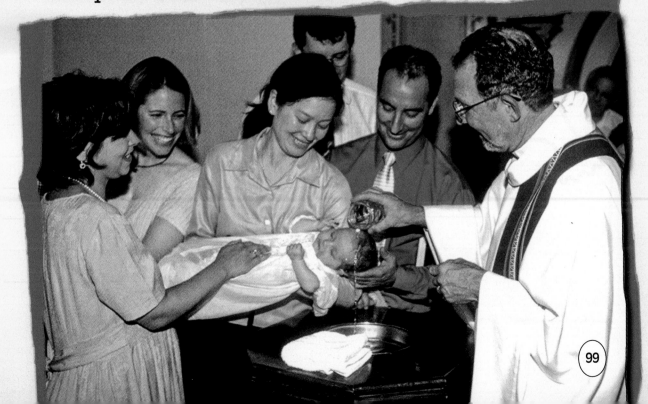

We Celebrate Confirmation

We celebrate Confirmation after we are baptized. At Confirmation the bishop, or the priest named by the bishop, rubs oil blessed by the Church on the front of our heads. As he rubs the oil, he says, "Be sealed with the gift of the Holy Spirit."

The bishop or priest then says, "Peace be with you." We respond, "And with your spirit." The Holy Spirit teaches us and helps us to live as followers of Jesus.

ACTIVITY *Finish this prayer to the Holy Spirit.*

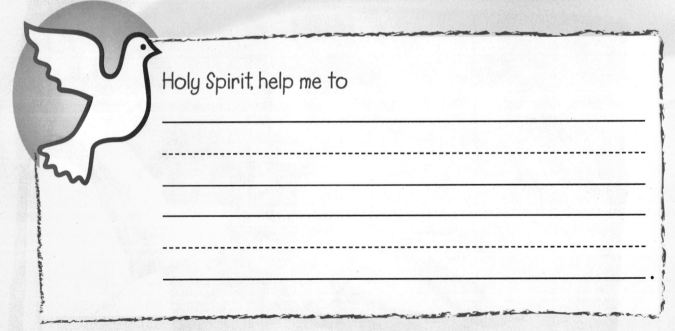

Holy Spirit, help me to

_____

- -

_____

_____

- -

_____ .

Project Star Fish

Jesus told us to be lights in the world. When we live our Baptism, we are lights in the world. The children of Divine Redeemer Parish in Colorado live their Baptism. They share God's love with children who have no families.

They gather clothing, toys, and school supplies. They share these and other things with children living in a home for children in the country of Jamaica. The children of Divine Redeemer Parish are bright lights for the children of Jamaica.

✝ Our Catholic Faith

Baptism Candle

At Baptism we receive a lighted candle. This reminds us that we are to live as followers of Jesus, who is the Light of the world. We are to be lights in the world.

QUESTION

How is your parish family a light in the world?

What Difference Does Faith Make in My Life?

At your Baptism God shared his love and life with you. You became a member of the Church. You received the gift of the Holy Spirit.

Write your name on the line. Read about what happened at your Baptism.

My Baptism

My name is _____.

I was baptized with _____.

I received the gift of the _____.

I received a lighted _____.

My Faith Choice

I will live as a follower of Jesus this week. I will

_____

_____.

Thank You, Lord

Water is God's gift to us. Water helps us to grow. Pray this prayer to thank God for the gift of water.

Leader: Lord, we thank you for the gift of water.

All: **Thank you, Lord.**

Leader: In Baptism water is a sign of new life in Jesus.

All: **Thank you, Lord.**

Leader: Come and dip your fingers in the water. Make the Sign of the Cross, and remember your Baptism.

All: **Amen!**

We Remember

Complete the sentences. Color the ◯ next to the best choice.

1. There are ____ sacraments.
   ◯ three   ◯ seven

2. ____ gave the Church the sacraments.
   ◯ Jesus   ◯ The saints

3. ____ is the first sacrament we receive.
   ◯ Eucharist   ◯ Baptism

To Help You Remember

1. In Baptism God shares his love and life with us.

2. In Baptism we receive the gift of the Holy Spirit.

3. In Confirmation we are sealed with the gift of the Holy Spirit to help us to live our Baptism.

This Week . . .

In chapter 11, "The Church's Celebrations," your child was introduced to the seven sacraments of the Church. Baptism is the first sacrament we receive. It is one of the three Sacraments of Christian Initiation, which are Baptism, Confirmation, and Eucharist. Through Baptism God makes us sharers in his life and love. We are joined to Christ, reborn as children of God, and receive the gift of the Holy Spirit. Original and personal sins are forgiven, and we become members of the Church, the Body of Christ. Confirmation strengthens the graces of Baptism.

For more on the teachings of the Catholic Church on the sacraments in general and on Baptism, see *Catechism of the Catholic Church* paragraph numbers 1113–1130 and 1210–1274.

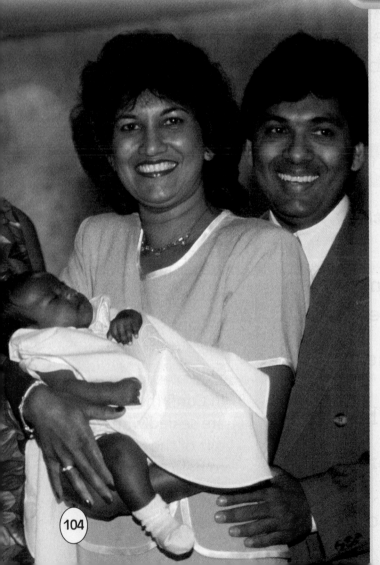

Sharing God's Word

Read together Matthew 5:14–16. Emphasize that at Baptism we are joined to Jesus, the Light of the world. We are to live our Baptism and be lights in the world.

Praying

In this chapter the children blessed themselves with water while praying the Sign of the Cross. Read and pray together the prayer on page 103.

Making a Difference

Choose one of the following activities to do as a family or design a similar activity of your own.

- Make thank-you cards for godparents. Thank your godparents for helping you grow in faith.

- Sign your child on her or his forehead with a small sign of the cross before your child leaves for school and at bedtime.

- Talk together about how your family lives their Baptism. Make a poster with the words "We Live Our Baptism." Draw pictures or write about how members of your family are lights in the world. Add words or drawings to the poster throughout the week.

For more ideas on ways your family can live your faith, visit the "Faith First for Families" page at **www.FaithFirst.com**. Click on "Family Prayer." Use the prayer as a family prayer this week.

Come, Follow Jesus

A Scripture Story

We Pray

Lord Jesus Christ, we believe in you. Amen.

What good news have you heard this week?

We all like to hear good news! The Bible tells us the Good News of God's love for us.

Who tells you about the Good News of God's love?

Bible Background

Faith Focus

Why do we share the Gospel with everyone?

Faith Words

Gospel
The Gospel is the Good News that Jesus told us about God's love.

The Good News of Jesus

Jesus told everyone the Good News of God's love. Jesus chose followers to help him share this Good News with all people.

Jesus chose Matthew to be one of his first followers. Matthew wrote about the Good News of Jesus. He wrote about this Good News in his **Gospel.** The word *gospel* means "Good News."

ACTIVITY Color the ❤s that show ways you can share the Good News of God's love.

The Good News of God's Love

 Tell people about Jesus.

 Say "Thank you" to someone who is kind to me.

Make a get-well card for a friend who is sick.

 Be rude to someone who is not kind to me.

Go and Tell the Good News

The followers of Jesus are called his disciples. The last story in Matthew's Gospel is about Jesus returning to his Father in heaven. In this story we hear the important command that Jesus gave to his disciples. Jesus told his disciples,

"Go to every land you can. Invite all people to be my disciples. Baptize them in the name of the Father, and of the Son, and of the Holy Spirit. Teach them what I have taught you."

Based on Matthew 28:19–20

How do you see Christians today doing what Jesus told his disciples to do?

Followers of Jesus Christ

The disciples of Jesus traveled to small villages and to large cities. They told everyone the Good News of Jesus Christ. They baptized people. They taught what Jesus taught them. Many people became followers of Jesus. People called the followers of Jesus Christians.

When we hear the Gospel, we come to know Jesus better. We grow in faith. We grow in our love for God and for other people.

ACTIVITY *Walk the maze to Jesus. Find and circle the things followers of Jesus share with others.*

We Follow Jesus

Saint Francis of Assisi

Saint Francis sang about the Good News of Jesus. God's love filled his heart.

Everywhere Saint Francis went he shared the Gospel. He told everyone that God is wonderful. God loves us so much that he gave us Jesus. Everything good in the world shows us how much God loves us.

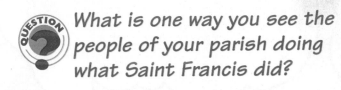 **What is one way you see the people of your parish doing what Saint Francis did?**

Our Catholic Faith

The Four Gospels

Saints Matthew, Mark, Luke, and John each wrote a Gospel about Jesus. The four Gospels are in the New Testament.

What Difference Does Faith Make in My Life?

You are a disciple of Jesus. The Holy Spirit helps you to tell people the Good News about Jesus.

Tell the Good News

Write what you want to tell other people about Jesus.

My Faith Choice

Check (✔) what you will do this week. I will share what I have written about Jesus with
- ❑ my parents
- ❑ my grandparents
- ❑ a friend
- ❑ someone at church

Lord, Help Us to Listen

At Mass we pray silently before we listen to the Gospel. We trace a small cross on our forehead, on our lips, and over our heart. Learn to pray in this new way.

Jesus, be in my thoughts,   **on my lips,**   **and in my heart.**

We Remember

Discover Jesus' Good News. Color the spaces with Xs red. Color the spaces with Ys other bright colors.

To Help You Remember

1. The Gospel is the Good News that Jesus told about God's love.
2. Jesus told his disciples to tell everyone the Good News he shared with them.
3. When we listen to the Gospel, we come to know Jesus better and to grow in faith.

This Week . . .

In chapter 12, "Come, Follow Jesus: A Scripture Story," your child learned that the Gospel is the Good News about Jesus. Matthew, Mark, Luke, and John are the four Evangelists, or Gospel writers. The last story in Matthew's Gospel is about Jesus' commissioning his disciples to preach the Gospel, to baptize, and to teach all people what he taught.

For more on the teachings of the Catholic Church on the writing of the Gospel and Jesus' commission of his disciples to baptize, teach, and make disciples of all nations, see *Catechism of the Catholic Church* paragraph numbers 124–133 and 849–856.

Sharing God's Word

Read together the Bible story in Matthew 28:19–20 about the command Jesus gave to the disciples or read the adaptation of the story on page 107. Emphasize that Jesus told the disciples to invite all people to be his disciples.

Praying

In this chapter your child prayed the prayer we pray at Mass before we listen to the Gospel. Practice and pray together the prayer on page 111.

Making a Difference

Choose one of the following activities to do as a family or design a similar activity of your own.

- Saint Francis of Assisi sang about the Good News of Jesus. Invite each family member to share their favorite song or hymn that tells about Jesus. Be sure everyone explains why the song or hymn is their favorite.

- Jesus told his disciples to announce the Good News of God's love to everyone. Choose one thing you can do to share that Good News with one another and with friends and neighbors.

- Invite each family member to share one thing they would like people to know about Jesus.

For more ideas on ways your family can live your faith, visit the "Faith First for Families" page at **www.FaithFirst.com**. Visit the "Reading Nook" with your child. Enjoy the story together.

We Celebrate Mass

We Pray

God, Father, Son, and Holy Spirit, we give you thanks and praise.

Amen.

What is one way that you have said thank you to someone?

We thank people in many ways. Our Church family thanks God in a special way at Mass.

What do you see and hear at Mass?

We Gather for Mass

Why does our Church family gather to celebrate Mass?

Faith Words

Mass
The Mass is the most important celebration of the Church.

Eucharist
The Eucharist is the sacrament in which we receive the Body and Blood of Christ.

We Gather as God's People

The **Mass** is the most important celebration of the Church. We gather as the People of God. We worship God. We listen to God's word. We celebrate and share in the **Eucharist.**

We begin the Mass by praying the Sign of the Cross. This reminds us of our Baptism. We remember that we belong to Jesus and are members of the Church.

 Name the people and things in the picture that you see at Mass.

We Listen to God's Word

We listen to readings from the Bible at every Mass. God tells us about his love for us. On Sunday we listen to three readings. The third reading is from the Gospel.

After the Gospel is read, the priest or deacon helps us to understand God's word. We come to know and love God. We learn ways to live as Jesus taught.

Next we tell God that we believe in him. Then we pray for other people and for ourselves.

Faith-Filled People

Priests

Priests are the bishop's coworkers. They lead us in the celebration of Mass. They teach us what Jesus taught. They help us to live as followers of Jesus.

ACTIVITY Write about or draw yourself living as Jesus taught.

Living the Gospel

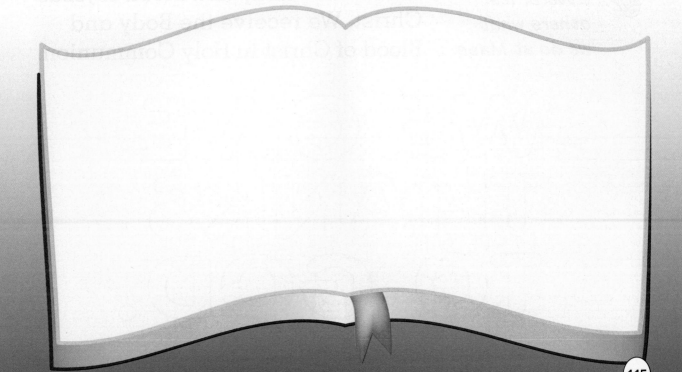

We Give Thanks to God

At Mass we celebrate the Eucharist. We give thanks to God. We remember and do what Jesus did at the Last Supper. The Last Supper is the meal that Jesus ate with his disciples on the night before he died.

At the Last Supper Jesus took bread and wine. He took the bread and said, "This is my body." He took the cup of wine and said, "This is my blood." Based on Matthew 26:26–28

At Mass the bread and wine become the Body and Blood of Jesus Christ. We receive the Body and Blood of Christ in Holy Communion.

ACTIVITY *Color the letters. Tell others what we do at Mass.*

WE GIVE THANKS TO GOD.

Love and Serve the Lord

At the end of Mass we are told, "Go in peace, glorifying the Lord by your life." The children of St. Mary's Parish who received first Holy Communion did that in a special way. They visited elderly people living in a nursing home.

The children spent time with the elderly people. They played a Bible board game together. It was their way of saying thank you for the gift of first Holy Communion. It was their way of sharing God's love with other people.

Our Catholic Faith

Peacemakers

Peacemakers share God's love with people. Jesus taught that God blesses peacemakers. Jesus said, "Blessed are the peacemakers, for they will be called children of God" (Matthew 5:9).

QUESTION ? *How can you share God's love with people?*

At Mass you listen to God's word. You learn ways to live as a follower of Jesus. You thank God.

Check (✔) the things you can do at Mass.

Thank You, God

☐ Pay attention.

☐ Listen to the readings.

☐ Pray aloud with my parish family.

☐ Sing songs to praise God.

☐ Say a thank-you prayer to God.

My Faith Choice

This week I will show my love for God. I will

_____

- -

_____ .

Thank You, God

We can pray quietly in our hearts and we can pray aloud.

Leader: Let us all remember Jesus. Think about Jesus. *(Pause)*

All: **Thank you, God.**

Leader: Think about what Jesus told us about God. *(Pause)*

All: **Thank you, God.**

Leader: Think about people who share God's love with you. *(Pause)*

All: **Thank you, God.**

We Remember

Draw a line to match the words with their meanings.

Words	Meanings
Last Supper	The celebration in which we listen to the word of God. We say thank you to God.
Mass	The sacrament in which we receive the Body and Blood of Christ.
Eucharist	The meal Jesus ate with his disciples on the night before he died.

To Help You Remember

1. At Mass we worship God.

2. At Mass we listen to readings from the Bible.

3. At Mass we celebrate and share the Eucharist.

This Week . . .

In chapter 13, "We Celebrate Mass," your child learned that the Mass is the most important celebration of the Church. During the Liturgy of the Word, we listen to the readings from the Bible. In the Liturgy of the Eucharist, we remember and do what Jesus did at the Last Supper. The bread and wine become the Body and Blood of Jesus. We receive the Body and Blood of Christ in Holy Communion.

For more on the teachings of the Catholic Church on the sacrament of the Eucharist, see *Catechism of the Catholic Church* paragraph numbers 1322–1405.

Sharing God's Word

Read together the Bible story in Matthew 26:26–29 about the Last Supper or read the adaptation of the story on page 116. Emphasize that at Mass the bread and wine become the Body and Blood of Christ.

Praying

In this chapter your child prayed a vocal prayer of thanksgiving, combining silent prayer and praying aloud. Read and pray together the prayer on page 119.

Making a Difference

Choose one of the following activities to do as a family or design a similar activity of your own.

- At the end of Mass we are dismissed with these or similar words, "Go in peace, glorifying the Lord by your life." Choose one thing your family can do together to love and serve the Lord this week.

- The Eucharist is the sacrament in which we receive the Body and Blood of Christ. Help your child become familiar with the word *Eucharist*. Write the word on a card and help your child practice saying "Eucharist."

- The tabernacle is the place where the Blessed Sacrament is reserved. Take the time this week to pray before the Blessed Sacrament.

For more ideas on ways your family can live your faith, visit the "Faith First for Families" page at **www.FaithFirst.com**. Click on "Bible Stories." Read and discuss the story with your child.

Jesus Feeds a Crowd
A Scripture Story

We Pray

Lord God, you always love us. Amen.

What foods are your family's favorites?

Healthy food helps us to grow. The Bible has many stories about Jesus sharing food with people.

What special food does our Church family share at Mass?

Bread, a symbol for the Eucharist

121

Bible Background

Faith Focus

Why did Jesus share food with others?

Faith Words

Galilee
Galilee was one of the main places where Jesus taught and helped people.

miracle
A miracle is something only God can do. It is a sign of God's love.

The Food of Jesus' Time

Many of the first disciples of Jesus lived in **Galilee.** Galilee was the place where Jesus did much of his teaching. He also helped many people who lived there.

Some people in Galilee were fishermen. They fished in the Sea of Galilee for their food. Other people were farmers. They grew fruit and barley. They made bread from the barley.

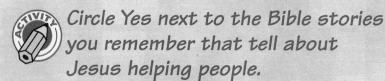 *Circle Yes next to the Bible stories you remember that tell about Jesus helping people.*

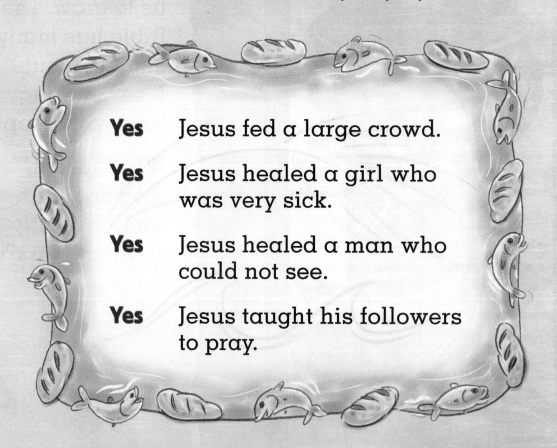

Yes Jesus fed a large crowd.

Yes Jesus healed a girl who was very sick.

Yes Jesus healed a man who could not see.

Yes Jesus taught his followers to pray.

Jesus Feeds the People

One time Jesus was teaching near the Sea of Galilee all day long. A very large crowd of people was listening to Jesus. This is what happened.

It became late and the people were hungry. But Jesus' followers only had five loaves of bread and two fish. Jesus took the bread and the fish and prayed. His followers gave the food to the people. Everyone ate until they were full.

Based on Matthew 14:15–16, 19–20

Jesus shared food with his followers. Jesus fed people to teach them about God's love.

ACTIVITY *Use the picture to tell a partner the story of Jesus feeding the people.*

Jesus Shares God's Love

The story of Jesus sharing the bread and fish tells about a **miracle.** A miracle is something only God can do. It is a special sign of God's love.

The story of Jesus feeding the people shows how Jesus shared God's love with the people. Jesus took care of the people.

Jesus asks us to take care of one another too. This is one way we share God's love with people.

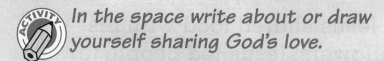

In the space write about or draw yourself sharing God's love.

Our Church Makes a Difference

Operation Rice Bowl

Christians share their blessings with the poor. We do this each year in a special way during Lent. We take part in Operation Rice Bowl.

Children share their allowance. Adults share their pay. Each family puts the money in a special box. At the end of Lent, they bring the box with the money to church. All the boxes are collected. The Church uses the money to help people. This is one way the Church shares God's love with people.

What is one way that you can share your blessings with people?

Our Catholic Faith

Grace

The gift of God's grace helps us to share God's love with people. The word *grace* means gift. It names the gift of God's life and love that God gives us. It also names the help that God gives us to live as children of God.

What Difference Does Faith Make in My Life?

Jesus fed the people to show that God cares for them. The Holy Spirit helps you to show God's love and care for others.

Check (✓) what you do to care for other people.

Caring for Others

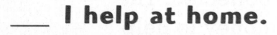

_____ I help at home.

_____ I play fairly.

_____ I am kind to my neighbors.

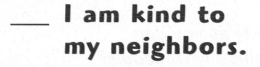

_____ I pray for people who need food.

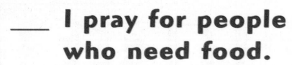

My Faith Choice

Choose one of the things you have checked. Try your best to do it often.

A Blessing Prayer

Blessing prayers tell God we know that all good things come from him. Pray this blessing prayer together.

Leader: Father, you care for everyone.

All: **Blessed be God.**

Leader: Jesus, you showed us how to care for people.

All: **Blessed be God.**

Leader: Holy Spirit, you help us to care for others.

All: **Blessed be God.**

God is Love

We Remember

Read each sentence about the story of Jesus feeding the people. Number the sentences in the order they happen in the story.

_____ Everyone ate until they were filled.

_____ Jesus took the five loaves and two fish and prayed.

_____ A large crowd was listening to Jesus. It was evening and they were hungry.

To Help You Remember

1. Jesus saw that the people were hungry and gave them all enough to eat.

2. Jesus showed people that God cares for them.

3. Jesus teaches us to care for people.

This Week . . .

In chapter 14, "Jesus Feeds a Crowd: A Scripture Story," your child listened to the story of Jesus feeding a large crowd with only five loaves of bread and two fish (Matthew 14:15–20). This story tells that Jesus took care of people to remind them of God's love for them. This story is one of the miracle stories in the Gospel. It reveals God's Providence, or God's loving care for people and all creation. This story teaches and invites us to care for others. When we do, we are signs of God's caring love for all people.

For more on the teachings of the Catholic Church on the miracles of Jesus and divine Providence, see *Catechism of the Catholic Church* paragraph numbers 302–308 and 547–550.

Sharing God's Word

Read together the Bible story in Matthew 14:15–20 about Jesus feeding the crowd or read the adaptation of the story on page 123. Emphasize that everyone ate until they were full. This is a sign of God's caring love for all people.

Praying

In this chapter your child prayed a blessing prayer. Read and pray together the prayer on page 127.

Making a Difference

Choose one of the following activities to do as a family or design a similar activity of your own.

- Make a loaf of homemade bread and eat it together. Talk about how good the fresh bread tastes. Imagine your family is in this lesson's Scripture story. Tell what it is like eating the bread the disciples gave you.

- Jesus fed the hungry people to show them that God loves and cares for them. Choose to do one thing this week to show people that God loves and cares for them.

- When you go grocery shopping this week, purchase food to donate to the local food pantry. Join with others to be a sign of God's loving care for all people.

For more ideas on ways your family can live your faith, visit the "Faith First for Families" page at **www.FaithFirst.com**. Click on "Family Prayer." Pray together this week.

A. The Best Word or Phrase

Complete the sentences. Color the circle next to the best choice.

1. Advent, Christmas, Lent, and ___ are all seasons of the Church year.

   ○ **Winter**   ○ **Easter**

2. Jesus gave the Church seven ___ to help us grow closer to God.

   ○ **commandments**   ○ **sacraments**

3. The first ___ of Jesus told everyone the Good News of God's love.

   ○ **family**   ○ **disciples**

4. Every Sunday the people of the Church gather to celebrate ___ .

   ○ **Confirmation**   ○ **Mass**

5. At the ___ , Jesus said, "This is my body" and "This is my blood."

   ○ **First Easter**   ○ **Last Supper**

B. Words about the Church Seasons

Use purple, green, or white to color the circle next to each Church season. Use the correct color for each season.

○ **Advent**   ○ **Easter**   ○ **Lent**

○ **Ordinary Time**   ○ **Christmas**

C. What I Learned

1. *What new thing did you learn about in this unit? Tell a partner.*

2. *Look at the list of faith words on page 88. Circle the ones that you know now.*

D. From a Scripture Story

Draw a picture or write about what happened in the Scripture story after Jesus prayed over the bread and fish.

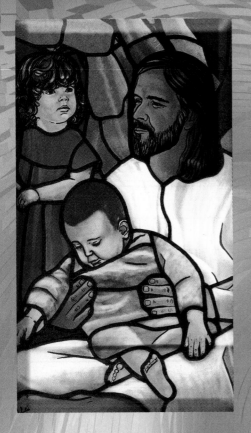

What do Christians do to live as children of God?

Getting Ready

What I Have Learned

What is something you know about the Ten Commandments?

_____

_____

_____

_____

Words to Know

Put an X next to the faith words you know. Put a ? next to the words you need to know more about.

Faith Words

_____ children of God

_____ marriage

_____ Great Commandment

_____ Ten Commandments

_____ worship

_____ respect

A Question I Have

What question would you like to ask about forgiving others?

_____

_____

_____

From a Scripture Story

Moses leading God's people

What do you know about Moses?

We Live as Children of God

We Pray

Loving God, you know each of us by name. Bless us with your love.
Amen.

What are some ways people differ from one another?

People have different skin colors. They speak different languages. The Bible tells us that all people are the same in one important way.

What is one way that all people are the same?

God Made Us

Faith Focus

What does it mean to be children of God?

Faith Words

children of God
All people are children of God. God created all people in his image.

glory
Glory is another word for praise.

QUESTION ? *What does this picture tell you about who are children of God?*

We Are Children of God

God created all people out of love. God created all people to know, love, and serve him. The Bible says,

God created people in his image. Based on Genesis 1:27

All people are part of God's family. We are **children of God.** Children of God love God and love one another. Our kind words and actions show others that we love them and care about them.

God Gives Us the Gift of Life

God is our loving Father. God shares the gift of his life with us. Children of God take very good care of the gift of life.

We respect and take care of the gift of our own lives. We respect and take care of the lives of other people.

 Write about or draw pictures that show how you can care for your own life and the life of someone else.

Caring for My Life

Caring for Another Person's Life

We Show Our Love for God

Jesus taught about God's love. Jesus taught that God wants us to be happy with him now and forever in heaven.

Underline one sentence in the second paragraph that tells one way you show your love for God.

God made us to know and to love him. Jesus showed us how to love God. We show our love for God when we help other people. We show our love for God when we pray. When we take care of creation, we are showing our love for God.

We give **glory** to God when we do these things. Children of God give glory and praise to God in all they do and say.

The Sisters of the Blessed Sacrament

Saint Katharine Drexel began the Sisters of the Blessed Sacrament. The Sisters of the Blessed Sacrament work with African-Americans and Native Americans. They work in schools and colleges. They work in cities and on the lands where Native Americans live.

The Sisters of the Blessed Sacrament continue the work begun by Saint Katharine Drexel. They treat all people as children of God. They teach others to treat all people with respect and fairness.

QUESTION *What are some of the ways you see people treating one another as children of God?*

Our Catholic Faith

Blessed Sacrament

The Blessed Sacrament is another name for the Eucharist. We keep the Blessed Sacrament in the tabernacle. We bring the Blessed Sacrament to people who are sick to receive Holy Communion.

What Difference Does Faith Make in My Life?

God made you and all people to be children of God. The Holy Spirit helps you to treat all people as children of God.

Trace the words of this prayer. Pray it with your class and with your family.

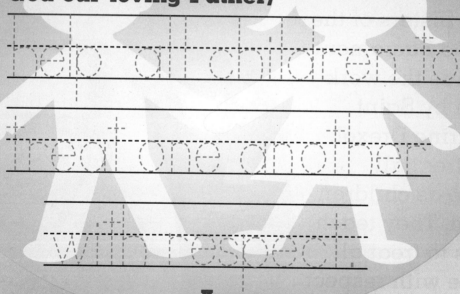

Praying for All Children

God our loving Father,

help all children to

treat one another

with respect

Amen.

My Faith Choice

Check (✓) how you will live as a child of God. This week I will

❑ be kind.

❑ pray.

❑ help my family.

❑ care for God's creation.

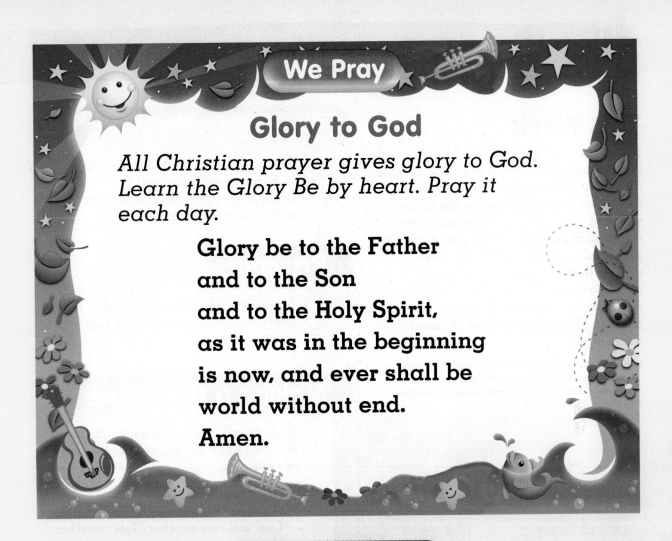

We Pray

Glory to God

All Christian prayer gives glory to God. Learn the Glory Be by heart. Pray it each day.

**Glory be to the Father
and to the Son
and to the Holy Spirit,
as it was in the beginning
is now, and ever shall be
world without end.
Amen.**

We Remember

Use this number code. Find out the important message about ourselves.

A	C	D	E	G	H	I	L
1	2	3	4	5	6	7	8

N	O	R	S	W
9	10	11	12	13

__ __   __ __ __   __ __ __
13 4   1 11 4   1 8 8

,

__ __ __ __   __ __ __ __ __ __ __ __
5 10 3 12   2 6 7 8 3 11 4 9

To Help You Remember

1. God made all people in his image.

2. God gives us the gift of life.

3. We are to take care of the gift of life.

This Week . . .

In chapter 15, "We Live as Children of God," your child learned that God created all people in the image and likeness of God. God created all people out of his infinite love. God calls all people to be responsible stewards of the gift of life. We are called to show our love for God, especially in the way we treat other people, no matter their race, social class, or nationality. We are to care for and treat our own life and the lives of all people with respect.

For more on the teachings of the Catholic Church on the dignity of all people as children of God, see *Catechism of the Catholic Church* paragraph numbers 355–361 and 1699–1709.

Sharing God's Word

Read together 1 John 3:1. Emphasize that in Baptism we are joined to Jesus and become adopted children of God. We are to live as Jesus taught.

Praying

In this chapter your child prayed the Glory Prayer. Read and pray together the prayer on page 139.

Making a Difference

Choose one of the following activities to do as a family or design a similar activity of your own.

- All people have the dignity of being children of God. Children of God love God and one another. Talk together about how your family can live as children of God. What kind words and actions show others that we love and care about them?

- When you take part in the celebration of Mass this week, look for the sanctuary lamp next to the tabernacle. Say a prayer together thanking Jesus for always being with your family.

- Look through a children's magazine or picture book with your child. Point out all the pictures that show people living as children of God.

For more ideas on ways your family can live your faith, visit the "Faith First for Families" page at **www.FaithFirst.com**. Click on "Contemporary Issues" for some interesting insights on living a life of faith in today's world.

We Live as a Family

We Pray

God, Father, Son, and Holy Spirit, bless our families. Amen.

What blessing would you like God to give your family?

We belong to a family. Our family is a blessing from God. Our family helps us to grow as children of God.

How does your family help you to grow as a child of God?

Family Love

How do our families help us to grow as children of God?

Faith Words

Matrimony

Matrimony is the sacrament Catholics celebrate when they get married.

marriage

A marriage is the lifelong promise of love made by a man and a woman to live as a family.

The Gift of Marriage

Sometimes a man and a woman love each other very much. They make a promise to love each other and to live as a family their whole lives. They get married. Catholics celebrate the sacrament of **Matrimony** when they get married.

A husband and a wife receive a wonderful gift from God in **marriage.** They receive the gift of children. They become parents. There are many different kinds of families. All families are called to love God and one another. They are to be signs of God's love in the world.

QUESTION How are the families in the pictures on these two pages signs of God's love?

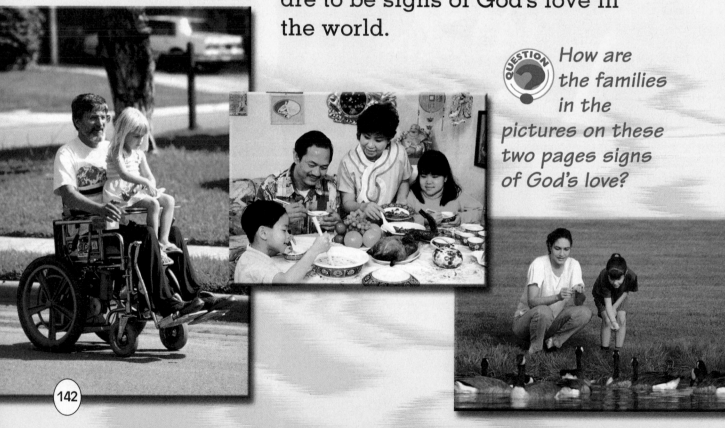

Elizabeth Seton

Saint Elizabeth Ann Seton is the first person born in America who was named a saint. Elizabeth and her husband, William, were the parents of five children.

Families Help One Another

A family is a blessing from God. Families are a sign of God's love. Christian families are a sign of Jesus' love for his followers.

Members of a family share their love with God and with one another. They pray together. They respect one another. They say and do kind things for one another. They take care of one another. They honor each other as children of God.

Write your family name. Tell how your family is a sign of God's love.

My Family Name

_____

_____.

God's Family

Each family is part of God's family. Our family helps us to grow in faith. Our family helps us to grow as Catholics.

Our family teaches us about the Holy Family. Mary, Joseph, and Jesus are the Holy Family. Our family teaches us about the saints.

Our family helps us to live our faith. It teaches us how to be part of our Church family. Our family teaches us to pray and to care for others as Jesus did.

The Holy Family

ACTIVITY

Check (✔) the ways a family can help one another to grow in faith and live as children of God.

☐ Pray as a family each day.

☐ Read the Bible together.

☐ Go to church.

Share one other thing a family can do.

Helping Families

Holy Family Day Home was started by the Sisters of the Holy Family. It is a place for children of parents who both need to work.

Holy Family Day Home is a place for young children to learn to respect themselves and others. The children play and learn during the day. Holy Family Day Home helps families to grow stronger.

Our Catholic Faith

The Family Church

Our families help us to know and love Jesus. They help us to live as disciples of Jesus. That is why we call our family "the Family Church" or "the Church of the home."

QUESTION *What are some things you do with your family that show respect for one another?*

What Difference Does Faith Make in My Life?

You are part of a family. The Holy Spirit helps you to share God's love with the members of your family.

Learn to sign these words. Teach the signs to your family. Share God's love with one another.

Sharing Family Love

God

loves

you.

My Faith Choice

This week I will share God's love with a member of my family. I will sign the message I learned.

We Pray

A Family Blessing

It is important to pray for our families. Let us ask God to bless the members of our families.

Leader: Lord God, show your wonderful love to all our families. Bless our grandparents,

All: **we ask you, Lord.**

Leader: Bless our parents,

All: **we ask you, Lord.**

Leader: Bless *(say the names silently in your heart),*

All: **we ask you, Lord.**

We Remember

Read this poem. Fill in the blanks with rhyming words.

Families, families, everywhere
show each other love and

_____

- -

_____ .

They tell us of God's love, you see.
God loves each of us, you and

_____

- -

_____ .

To Help You Remember

1. Christian families are signs of Jesus' love for his followers.

2. Members of a family share their love for God with one another.

3. Our family helps us to live our faith.

This Week . . .

In chapter 16, "We Live as a Family," your child learned that God invites men and women to share their love for him and for one another forever in marriage. Matrimony is the sacrament Catholics celebrate when they marry. Families are signs of God's love. Families are the primary place where parents and children experience and grow in faith, hope, and love. Christian families are signs of Jesus' love for the Church.

For more on the teachings of the Catholic Church on the sacrament of Matrimony and Christian family life, see *Catechism of the Catholic Church* paragraph numbers 1601–1658 and 2197–2233.

Sharing God's Word

Read together the Bible story in Luke 2:41–52 about the finding of Jesus in the Temple in Jerusalem when he was twelve years old. Emphasize that in the Holy Family, Jesus grew in love for God and for his family.

Praying

In this chapter your child learned a family blessing prayer. Read and pray together the prayer on page 147.

Making a Difference

Choose one of the following activities to do as a family or design a similar activity of your own.

- When we pray as a family, we show that our family loves God. Make an extra effort this week to pray together at least once a day.

- Families are signs of God's love. Talk about the many ways your family is a sign of God's love. When do you pray together? When do you do kind things for one another? Choose one thing you will do this week to share God's love with one another.

- Family members help one another grow in faith. They encourage and support one another to live as Jesus taught. Share with one another how you help each other grow in faith.

For more ideas on ways your family can live your faith, visit the "Faith First for Families" page at **www.FaithFirst.com**. Click on "Gospel Reflections." Talk about the Gospel story with your child. Help each other grow in faith.

We Live as a Community

We Pray

O Lord, our God, help us to live together in peace. Amen.

Where does your family live?

Families live in a town or a city and in the country. We follow rules to help us to live together. Our Church community helps us to live together too.

What are some of the rules of the Church?

All People Belong to God's Family

Faith Focus

What does it mean to live the Great Commandment?

Faith Words

community
A community is a group of people who respect and care for one another.

Great Commandment
The Great Commandment is to love God above all else and to love others as we love ourselves.

We Are All Special

God makes each of us different. God blesses each of us with special gifts. We respect each other's gifts. God asks us to use our gifts to live as a **community**. A community is a group of people who respect and care for one another. We all belong to the community of God's people.

QUESTION *How are the children in the pictures sharing their gifts?*

Rules Help Us

Rules help us to live together in a community. They help us to respect one another. The rules a community makes are called laws. A good law helps a community to live together in peace.

God has laws for us too. God's laws help us to know right and wrong. They help us to make good choices. They help us to respect one another and to care for one another. God's laws help us to live as children of God.

ACTIVITY Follow the road in the picture. Circle a favorite place. Write one way you can live as a child of God there.

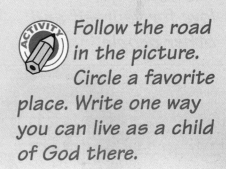

The Great Commandment

God wants all people to love him with their whole heart. He wants all people to love and respect others as they love themselves. We call this the **Great Commandment,** or the Great Law of God. The Great Commandment helps us to live as the community of God's people.

Jesus showed us how to live the Great Commandment. Jesus gave us the gift of the Church. The Church helps us to live the Great Commandment.

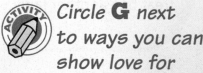 *Circle* **G** *next to ways you can show love for God. Circle* **P** *next to ways you can show love for yourself and other people.*

Living the Great Commandment

G   P   Pray

G   P   Say kind words

G   P   Act fairly

G   P   Take part in Mass

G   P   Forgive others

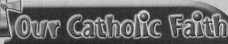

Religious Vows

Members of religious communities make special promises, or vows. The promises and vows help them to love God more than all else. The promises and vows help them to love people as Jesus taught us to do.

Living the Great Commandment

All the members of the Church are called to live the Great Commandment. God calls some members of the Church to live in religious communities. They are called religious sisters and brothers, religious priests and deacons. They live, work, and pray together. Members of religious communities help one another to live the Great Commandment.

 How are the people in the pictures living the Great Commandment?

What Difference Does Faith Make in My Life?

The Holy Spirit helps you to live as a good member of your community.

Finish each sentence. Write what you can do to live as a good member of your community.

Living God's Laws

_____

1. I can share my _____.

_____

2. I can help by _____.

_____

3. I can pray for _____.

My Faith Choice

Write Yes next to one thing you wrote above. Do it this week to live the Great Commandment.

Praying the Bible

This prayer is part of Psalm 25. Learn the words by heart. Pray them each day. Ask God to teach and to help you to live the Great Commandment.

**LORD God, teach me your way.
You are my God and Savior.**

Based on Psalm 25:4 and 5

We Remember

Find and circle the three words hidden in the puzzle. Share with a partner what each word tells about the Great Commandment.

GOD   LOVE   PEOPLE

L H L O V E T Y
Q L P G O D M U
P E O P L E B D

To Help You Remember

1. The Great Commandment helps us to love God and to love other people as we love ourselves.

2. The Great Commandment helps us to follow Jesus.

3. The Great Commandment helps us to live as good members of our community.

This Week . . .

In chapter 17, "We Live as a Community," your child learned that God created people to live in community. Each of us is called by God to share our gifts and blessings with others. This helps us build good communities. Communities make laws to help people live together in peace. God gives us laws to help us show our love for God, for ourselves, and for other people. The Great Commandment is the summary of all God's laws. The Church helps us live God's Law and the good laws that communities make.

For more on the teachings of the Catholic Church on the nature of the human community and the responsibilities of being a part of a community, see *Catechism of the Catholic Church* paragraph numbers 1877–1942, 1949–1974, and 2234–2246.

Sharing God's Word

Read together the Bible story in Matthew 22:34–40 about Jesus teaching the Great Commandment. Emphasize that the Great Commandment has two parts. We are to love God and we are to love all people as we love ourselves.

Praying

In this chapter your child prayed using the Bible. Read and pray together the prayer on page 155.

Making a Difference

Choose one of the following activities to do as a family or design a similar activity of your own.

- Rules help us live together. Talk about your family rules and how they help you live together.

- Choose an activity to do this week to live the Great Commandment.

- Talk about the special gifts each person brings to your family. For example, one person might be well organized and another person might have a good sense of humor. Give examples of how using those gifts is a blessing for your family.

For more ideas on ways your family can live your faith, visit the "Faith First for Families" page at www.FaithFirst.com. Click on "Games." Invite your child to choose their favorite game. Play it together.

Moses Leads God's People
A Scripture Story

We Pray

God our loving Father, you always care for us. Help us to care for one another. Amen.

Who are some of the people who care for you?

God gives us our family to care for us. The Bible tells us that God gives us other people to care for us.

Who do you know in the Bible who cared for God's people?

The land Moses and God's people traveled

Bible Background

Faith Focus

What does the story of Moses tell us about God's love?

Faith Words

Moses

God chose Moses to be a leader of God's people.

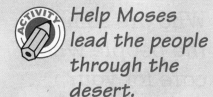

Help Moses lead the people through the desert.

A Special Leader

God chooses leaders to take care of his people. A long, long time ago, God chose **Moses** to be a leader of God's people. He chose Moses to lead his people through the desert to their new homeland.

Moses was afraid he would not be able to take care of God's people. But God told Moses he would always be with him to help him.

Moses trusted God. He listened to God and learned how to care for God's people.

Moses Leads God's People

In the Bible, we read this story about Moses.

God told Moses to take his people to a new land. During the trip the people traveled through the desert. The people became very thirsty and hungry.

The people complained to Moses. Moses prayed to God. The next morning, the ground was covered with food that fell from heaven. The food tasted like bread. Everyone had enough to eat!

Based on Exodus 15:22, 24; 16:2–4, 13–16

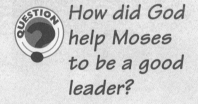 *How did God help Moses to be a good leader?*

When Moses prayed for God's people, he was acting as a good leader.

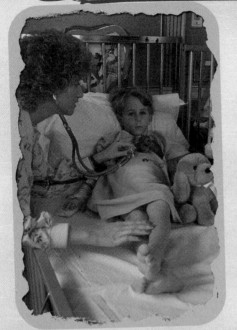

God Cares for His People

God showed Moses and his people the way to the new land where they would live. God gave them food when they were hungry. He watched over them and kept them safe.

The story of Moses shows us God's great love for his people. God always cares for his people.

We are God's people. God always takes care of us because he loves us. Everywhere we can see signs of God's love.

 Draw a picture of someone being a sign of God's love for you.

Our Church Makes a Difference

Caring for People

The teenagers of Holy Trinity Parish babysitter service are signs of God's love. While they are babysitting, the teenagers tell the children Bible stories. They pray with the children when they feed them and when they put them to bed, even for a nap.

The Holy Trinity babysitters do these things because of their love for God. Like Moses, they are signs that God cares for his people.

 Who are some of the people who care for you? How are they signs of God's caring love for you?

What Difference Does Faith Make in My Life?

When you care for others, you are a sign of God's caring love for all people.

Fill in this coupon to tell how you will care for someone this week.

I Care for You Coupon

This coupon is for _____

_____

_____ .

I will show my care for you this week by _____

_____

_____

_____

_____ .

My Faith Choice

This week I will do what I wrote in the coupon.

We Pray

A Vocation Prayer

Leader: God calls everyone to be a sign that he cares for all people. This calling from God is our vocation. Let us pray together.

All: God, I know you will call us for special work in our life. Help us to follow Jesus each day and be ready to answer your call. Amen.

Come, follow me

We Remember

Read each sentence from the Bible story about Moses. Number the sentences in the order they happened in the story.

_____ The people complained to Moses.

_____ God told Moses to take his people to a new land.

_____ The people had enough to eat.

_____ Moses prayed to God.

To Help You Remember

1. God chooses special people to care for his people.

2. God chose Moses to care for God's people.

3. God always chooses people to care for us. These people are signs of God's caring love for us.

This Week . . .

In chapter 18, "Moses Leads God's People: A Scripture Story," your child learned that throughout the ages God has always chosen leaders to care for his people. Moses led the Hebrews, or Israelites, out of slavery in Egypt into freedom in the new land God had promised them. During this journey to the Promised Land, which is called the Exodus, God fed his people with manna. This reveals that God always cares for his people. We call God's constant, never-ending, loving care for all people divine Providence.

For more on the teachings of the Catholic Church on the prayer of Moses and divine Providence, see *Catechism of the Catholic Church* paragraph numbers 302–308, 1094, 1334, and 2574–2577.

Sharing God's Word

Read together the Bible story in Exodus 15:22–24 and Exodus 16:2–16 about Moses leading the Hebrews through the desert, or you can read the adaptation of the story on page 159. Emphasize that God told Moses that he would always be with him to help him. God always cares for his people.

Praying

In this chapter your child prayed a greeting that we say at the beginning of Mass. Read and pray together the prayer on page 163.

Making a Difference

Choose one of the following activities to do as a family or design a similar activity of your own.

- When you take part in the celebration of Mass this week, pay close attention to the greeting prayer at the beginning of Mass. Use it when a family member leaves or returns home.

- Talk about all the people who care for your family and what they do for you. Thank God for these wonderful people. You might also like to send thank-you notes to some of these people.

- Draw a picture of the people following Moses across the desert. Display the picture where it can help your family remember that God is always with you.

For more ideas on ways your family can live your faith, visit the "Faith First for Families" page at **www.FaithFirst.com**. Click on "Just for Parents." Reflect on a monthly article discussing parental issues and concerns.

We Love God

We Pray

Lord God,
we adore you.
We worship
you.   Amen.

*What are some
good rules for a
family?*

Rules help us
to care for
ourselves and
others. The Ten
Commandments
are rules that God
gave us. They
teach us to live as
children of God.

*What is one
of the Ten
Commandments?*

God's Commandments Help Us

Faith Focus

Why did God give us the Ten Commandments?

Faith Words

Ten Commandments
The Ten Commandments are the laws God has given us to help us to live as children of God.

worship
We worship God when we love and honor God more than anyone and anything else.

The Ten Commandments

We follow rules at home, at school, and in our community. These rules help us to care for ourselves, for others, and for creation.

God gave us rules to help us to live as children of God. God's rules are called commandments.

In the Bible we learn that God has given us the **Ten Commandments.** The Ten Commandments help us to live as children of God. They tell us to love God and others. They tell us to care for ourselves and for all creation.

 Write one way you can show your love for God. Write one way you can show your love for your family.

Jesus Teaches Us

Jesus taught us to live the Ten Commandments. Jesus showed us how to love God. Jesus prayed to his Father. He always did what God the Father asked him to do.

Jesus showed us how to love one another. He was kind to everyone. Jesus told us to treat people as he did. He said,

"I give you this new commandment. You are to love one another as I have loved you."

Based on John 13:34

QUESTION *How are the people in the pictures showing their love for God and their love for people?*

We Love God

The Ten Commandments tell us ways to show our love for God. We are to **worship** only God. We love and honor God more than anything and anyone else.

We honor God. We speak God's name with love and respect.

We give thanks and praise to God for all he has done for us. Every Sunday we gather with our Church family for Mass.

 Thank God for all he has done for you. Use words and pictures.

Thank you, God, for . . .

Our Church Makes a Difference

Christians Build Churches

Catholics gather in churches to worship God. Our churches are signs of our faith in God. Our churches show we love God above all else.

We give our churches names. The name *Holy Trinity Catholic Church* tells about our faith in God. The members of our Church help one another to love God with all our heart.

QUESTION What is the name of your parish church? How do the people of your parish help you to love God?

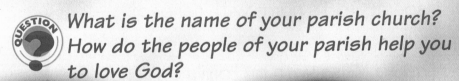

Our Catholic Faith

Cathedrals

The cathedral is the bishop's church. The name of the pope's cathedral is Saint John Lateran.

What Difference Does Faith Make in My Life?

The Holy Spirit helps you to show your love for God.

Draw a 😊 *next to the ways you can show your love for God.*

I Love God

I can pray.

I can speak God's name with respect.

I can go to Mass with my family on Sundays.

I can thank God for all his blessings.

_____

- -

I can _____.

My Faith Choice

Look at the smiley faces you drew. Check (✔) the 😊 that tells what you will do this week.

An Act of Love

An act of love is a prayer. When we pray an act of love, we tell God we love him more than anyone or anything.

O my God, you created me.

You share your love with me.

You are all-good.

I love you with my whole heart.

Amen.

We Remember

Draw lines to match the words in Column A with their meanings in Column B.

Column A

1. Honor God

2. Worship God

3. Thank God

Column B

a. Take part in Mass on Sundays.

b. Speak God's name with love and respect.

c. Love God above all else.

To Help You Remember

1. The Ten Commandments teach us to worship God.

2. The Ten Commandments teach us to speak God's name with love and respect.

3. The Ten Commandments teach us to take part in Mass on Sundays.

This Week . . .

In chapter 19, "We Love God," your child learned about the Ten Commandments. The Ten Commandments tell us ways to live the Great Commandment. The First, Second, and Third Commandments tell us to love, honor, and worship God above all else. Jesus taught us to live the Ten Commandments. We are to love God and people as Jesus taught.

For more on the teachings of the Catholic Church on the Ten Commandments and, in particular, the first three Commandments, see *Catechism of the Catholic Church* paragraph numbers 2052–2074, and First Commandment (2083–2132), Second Commandment (2142–2159), and Third Commandment (2168–2188).

Sharing God's Word

Read together the Bible story in John 13:34–35 in which Jesus teaches his disciples the New Commandment or you can read an adaptation of the story on page 167. Emphasize that Jesus by his example showed us how to love God and one another.

Praying

In this chapter your child prayed an act of love. Read and pray together the prayer on page 171.

Making a Difference

Choose one of the following activities to do as a family or design a similar activity of your own.

- Talk about the ways each family member is alike and how each is different. Emphasize that God created each person as a unique individual person and loves each person in a special way.

- When you gather for dinner this week, begin by inviting each person to share one thing they did that day to show their love for God.

- Make a banner using the words "Love God, Love Others, Love Yourself." Display the banner where it can remind your family to live the Ten Commandments.

For more ideas on ways your family can live your faith, visit the "Faith First for Families" page at **www.FaithFirst.com**. Visit "Make a Difference" and discover ways to live your faith as a family.

We Love Others

We Pray

God of love,
teach us to love
one another.
Amen.

*What are some of
the ways you show
love for others?*

We show our love
for others when we
respect them. The
Commandments
teach us to respect
ourselves and
others.

*What is one way the
Commandments
teach us to respect
ourselves and
others?*

We Respect People

Faith Focus

What do the Ten Commandments teach about respect?

Faith Words

respect
We show people respect when we love them because they are children of God.

honor
We honor people when we treat them with great respect.

Showing Respect

The Ten Commandments tell us to **respect** other people and ourselves. Showing respect is a way to show love. We show respect when we treat and **honor** other people and ourselves as children of God.

We show respect to people in many ways. We listen carefully to one another. We are polite and kind. We are fair to one another.

We show respect to ourselves in many ways. We take care of our bodies. We act safely.

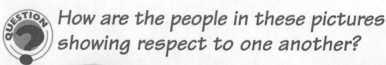

How are the people in these pictures showing respect to one another?

Respecting Others

The Ten Commandments tell us to respect what belongs to us and to other people. We are to take good care of the things we have. We are to share our things to help others.

We show respect for what belongs to others when we ask before we borrow their things. We return the things that we borrow. We do not steal.

Faith-Filled People

Vincent de Paul

Saint Vincent de Paul treated all people with respect. He cared for people no one cared about. The Church celebrates the feast day of Saint Vincent de Paul on September 27.

ACTIVITY Write or draw one way you can show respect for people.

Telling the Truth

The Ten Commandments teach us to be honest. We are honest when we tell the truth. Lying shows we do not respect ourselves and other people.

It is important to tell the truth. When we tell the truth, we show respect for ourselves and other people. People trust us.

ACTIVITY *Imagine you are in the story. Write what you would say.*

Our Church Makes a Difference

Saint Vincent de Paul Society

People in many parishes continue the work of Saint Vincent de Paul. They are members of the Saint Vincent de Paul Society.

The members of the Saint Vincent de Paul Society show respect and love for people in many ways. They help families who cannot buy food or clothes or pay their rent. They help people to visit doctors and dentists. They run camps in the summertime so children can have a vacation.

QUESTION *What are some of the ways you see people being kind to one another? Why do acts of kindness show we respect people?*

What Difference Does Faith Make in My Life?

When you are kind and fair, you treat people with respect. You love people as Jesus taught.

Fill in the blanks in the story.

Showing Respect

I am working with _____ to make

_{your friend's name}

a poster. I ask another friend, "May we please

borrow your markers? We will take good

_____

_____ of them." When we are finished,

we will return the markers and say,

"_____ _____ "

_____ _____

_____ _____ .

My Faith Choice

Check (✔) ways you will show respect for other people.

- ❑ Tell the truth.
- ❑ Be rude and mean.
- ❑ Share my things.
- ❑ Play safely.

We Pray

We Pray for One Another

We pray for one another. This shows we care about and love one another.

Leader: God, you love us. As Jesus did, we pray for one another. For people who are hungry,

All: **Lord, hear our prayer.**

Leader: For people who are sick,

All: **Lord, hear our prayer.**

Leader: Everyone pray quietly for someone. *(Pause.)*

All: **Lord, hear our prayer.**

We Remember

Read each sentence. Circle Yes if the sentence is true. Circle No if it is not true.

1. **Respecting others is a way to show love.**   Yes   No

2. **Listening to one another shows respect.**   Yes   No

3. **Taking care of what belongs to others shows respect.**   Yes   No

4. **Telling lies shows respect.**   Yes   No

To Help You Remember

1. The Ten Commandments tell us to show respect for others and for ourselves.

2. Showing respect is a sign of love.

3. When we live the Ten Commandments, we treat one another as children of God.

This Week . . .

In chapter 20, "We Love Others," your child learned that the Commandments tell us to love and respect other people, ourselves, and all God's creation. The last seven Commandments name the ways we are to live the second part of the Great Commandment and truly live as children of God.

For more on the teachings of the Catholic Church on the Ten Commandments and in particular the last seven Commandments, see *Catechism of the Catholic Church* paragraph numbers 2052–2074 and Fourth Commandment (paragraph numbers 2196–2246), Fifth Commandment (2258–2317), Sixth Commandment (2331–2391), Seventh Commandment (2401–2449), Eighth Commandment (2464–2503), Ninth Commandment (2514–2527), and Tenth Commandment (2534–2550).

Sharing God's Word

Read together the Bible story in Acts of the Apostles 2:42–47. Emphasize that this story tells about the first Christians living the Commandments as Jesus taught.

Praying

In this chapter your child prayed for others. This is called a prayer of intercession. Read and pray together the prayer on page 179.

Making a Difference

Choose one of the following activities to do as a family or design a similar activity of your own.

• Put each family member's name in a bowl. Have each person draw a name. Be sure that no one has drawn their own name. Within the week, each person is to do something for the person whose name they drew.

• Read together a children's book about treating people with respect. Discuss why showing respect is at the heart of our love for others.

• Identify and name ways your family shows respect for one another. For example, when you use kind words with each other or take good care of each other's belongings or cooperate with each other, and so on.

For more ideas on ways your family can live your faith, visit the "Faith First for Families" page at **www.FaithFirst.com**. This week pay special attention to "Questions Kids Ask."

We Love Through Forgiveness

We Pray

My God,
I am sorry for
choosing to do
wrong. Help
me to live as
your child.
            Amen.

Who has forgiven
you? Who have
you forgiven?

Forgiving others is
a sign of our love
for one another.
Christians show
their love by
forgiving one
another.

What did Jesus
teach us about
forgiveness?

181

Forgiving Others

Faith Focus

Why is it important to say "I am sorry" when we choose to do or say something that is wrong?

Faith Words

sin
Sin is choosing to do or say something we know is against God's laws.

Making Choices

We use words and actions to help others. Sometimes we choose to use our words and actions to hurt others. When we do, we are not obeying God. We **sin.**

Sin is choosing to do or say something we know is against God's laws. When we sin, we turn away from God's love.

Sin is choosing not to love others as Jesus taught us. Sin hurts our friendship with God and with other people.

QUESTION *What do these pictures show about making good or bad choices?*

Asking for Forgiveness

We feel sorry when we sin. We want to be forgiven. We want to make up for our sin.

We need to say we are sorry to God when we sin. We tell God we are sorry. We ask for forgiveness because we love God. God will always forgive us because he loves us.

We need to say we are sorry to the people we hurt by our sin. We need to ask for forgiveness. We want everything to be right again.

 Circle the bubbles with the words that show sorrow or forgiveness.

Leave me alone.

I'm sorry.

It's my fault.

Let's be friends.

Go away.

Faith-Filled People

John Vianney

Saint John Vianney was a priest. He treated people who were sorry for their sins with kindness and respect. Railroad tracks were built to his town because so many people wanted to come to him to receive forgiveness for their sins. The Church celebrates the feast day of Saint John Vianney on August 4.

Forgiving Others

Jesus tells us to forgive people who hurt us. He tells us to forgive them over and over again. He said,

"You are to forgive others who sin against you over and over again." Based on Matthew 18:21–22

Sometimes it is not easy to do what Jesus wants us to do. Sometimes we do not feel like forgiving people who hurt us. When we might not want to forgive others, the Holy Spirit helps us.

We open our hearts with love when we forgive others. We show our love for God and for one another. We are peacemakers.

ACTIVITY Draw a picture of yourself showing forgiveness.

The Pope Forgives

Pope John Paul II was riding in the back of his car. He was greeting and waving to people.

A man came out of the crowd and shot at the pope. The pope was hurt but soon got better.

The pope went to the prison and visited the man who shot him. He put his arms around the man and forgave him. The pope made peace with the man who hurt him. He showed us what Jesus wants us to do.

QUESTION *What are some of the ways you see people forgiving those who hurt them?*

Our Catholic Faith

Sign of Peace

Each Sunday at Mass, we shake hands or share another sign of peace with one another. This shows we want to forgive those who hurt us. We want to live together as the one family of God.

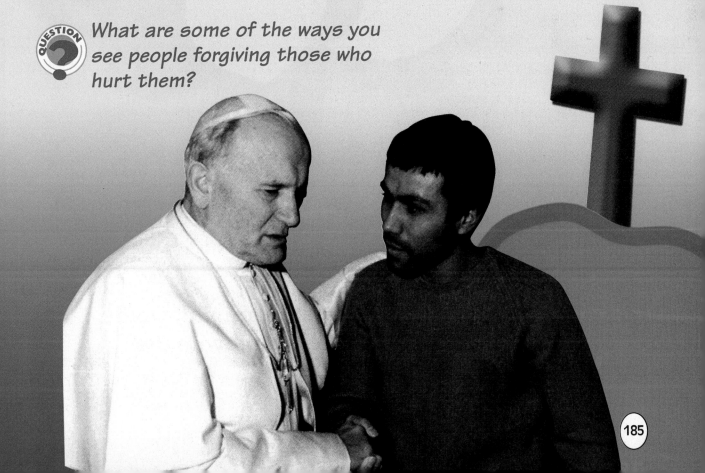

What Difference Does Faith Make in My Life?

The Holy Spirit teaches and helps you to forgive and to ask for forgiveness. When you forgive someone, it brings peace.

Forgiving Tree

In the leaves write words or draw actions that show forgiveness.

 My Faith Choice

This week I will use the forgiving words or actions that I wrote or drew in the "Forgiving Tree."

Prayer of Mercy

At the beginning of Mass, we ask God for his mercy. The word mercy reminds us that forgiveness is a gift of love.

Leader: Lord, have mercy.

All: **Lord, have mercy.**

Leader: Christ, have mercy.

All: **Christ, have mercy.**

Leader: Lord, have mercy.

All: **Lord, have mercy.**

We Remember

Discover a way Jesus tells us to be a sign of God's love. Color the spaces with a ♥ one color. Color the other spaces with other colors.

To Help You Remember

1. Sin hurts our friendship with God and other people.

2. When we say we are sorry, we show we love God and others.

3. When we say we are sorry, we ask for forgiveness from God and from others.

This Week . . .

In chapter 21, "We Love Through Forgiveness," your child was introduced to the concepts of sin and forgiveness. People can make choices to help others as well as make choices to hurt others. They can choose to do or say what they know is against the will of God. They can make choices to live or not to live by the Great Commandment. People can sin. Sin always hurts our relationship with God and with other people. When we sin, we need to say we are sorry both to God and to those we hurt. We need to ask for forgiveness. We need to reconcile our relationships with God and with people.

For more on the teachings of the Catholic Church on sin and forgiveness, see *Catechism of the Catholic Church* paragraph numbers 1420–1484 and 1846–1869.

Sharing God's Word

Read together the Bible story in Matthew 18:21–35 about the parable of the Unforgiving Servant. Emphasize that Jesus teaches us that we are to forgive others over and over again as God always forgives us when we are truly sorry for our sins.

Praying

In this chapter your child prayed a prayer of mercy. Read and pray together the prayer on page 187.

Making a Difference

Choose one of the following activities to do as a family or design a similar activity of your own.

- When you participate in the celebration of Mass this week, pay close attention to the prayer of mercy that we pray at the beginning of Mass. Remember that the word *mercy* reminds us that God's forgiveness is a gift of his love.

- Name ways people show that they are sorry. Talk about ways members of your family can both show one another forgiveness and accept forgiveness from one another.

- The sign of peace at Mass is a sign of love, friendship, and forgiveness. Share a sign of peace with one another. Show your willingness both to forgive and to accept forgiveness from one another.

For more ideas on ways your family can live your faith, visit the "Faith First for Families" page at **www.FaithFirst.com**. Click on "Family Prayer." Use the prayer during your family prayer time this week.

Jesus and the Children

A Scripture Story

We Pray

Holy Mary, mother of Jesus, pray for us and for all the world's children.

Amen.

How do people show that they are friends?

Getting an invitation to a party is a sign that someone is our friend. The Bible tells us that Jesus invites us to be his friends.

How do we know Jesus wants us to be his friends?

Bible Background

Faith Focus

Why are all children so special to Jesus?

Faith Words

kingdom of God
The kingdom of God is the kingdom of heaven.

Everyone Is Special to God

Jesus showed that every person is special. He showed that God loves everyone. Jesus treated everyone as a child of God. He cured people who were sick. He was kind to people who others did not like. Jesus forgave people who sinned. He loved those who wanted to hurt him.

QUESTION ? *How are the people in the pictures treating one another as children of God?*

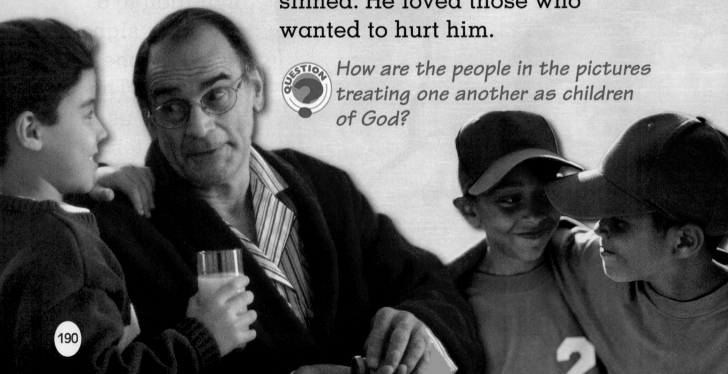

Reading the Word of God

Jesus and the Children

Here is a story from the Bible. It tells about Jesus inviting children to come to him.

People brought their children to Jesus. But the disciples told them to go away. Jesus said, "Let the children come to me." Then he blessed the children.

Based on Mark 10:13–14, 16

Jesus invites all people to come to him. All people are invited to live in the **kingdom of God.** The kingdom of God is heaven.

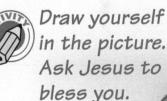 Draw yourself in the picture. Ask Jesus to bless you.

We Are Children of God

In the Bible story Jesus taught that all children are special to God. Some children have big, bright eyes. Others have a happy smile. Some are very quiet. Others talk all the time. All children are very different. Our differences show how special we are.

We treat all people as children of God. We do our best to live as children of God. We trust and love God with our whole heart.

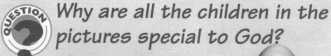 *Why are all the children in the pictures special to God?*

Our Church Makes a Difference

Children Helping Children

The children who belong to the Holy Childhood Association help children all over the world. They pray for other children. They give money to help other children. This money helps to build schools and homes. It helps nurses and doctors to care for children.

No matter where children live, they are children of God. No matter what skin color children have or what language they speak, all children are children of God.

 What are some of the ways you can help other children?

Our Catholic Faith

Children's Choir

Children help out in their parishes. One way they help is by singing in the children's choir. This shows that children have a special work to do in the Church.

What Difference Does Faith Make in My Life?

Jesus loves you. Jesus loves all children. The Holy Spirit helps you to share Jesus' love for them.

Use words and pictures to make an "I Care" button.

"I Care"

My Faith Choice

 Underline one way you will treat others as children of God. This week I will

1. invite a classmate to play with me.
2. tell my family I love them.
3. help out at home.

We Pray

Let the Children Come to Me

Our imagination can help us to pray. Our imagination helps us to be with Jesus. It can help us to talk to Jesus and to listen to him.

1. Sit quietly in a comfortable position.

2. Turn to page 191. Look at the picture and imagine that you are with your family and are going to see Jesus.

3. Imagine that you are talking and listening to Jesus with the other children.

4. Spend a minute quietly listening to what Jesus might be saying to you.

We Remember

Find and circle the four words hidden in the puzzle. Use the words to tell a friend how special they are to God.

Jesus	blesses	children	love

```
Q R T L B L E S S E S
Z W R B L L O V E X T
A B K C H I L D R E N
J E S U S M C S T R D
```

To Help You Remember

1. God loves all people.

2. God wants all people to come to him.

3. God wants us to live in the kingdom of heaven.

This Week . . .

In chapter 22, "Jesus and the Children: A Scripture Story," your child listened to the story of Jesus inviting the children to come to him. When the disciples told the people to leave Jesus alone, Jesus invited them to bring their children to him. After blessing the children, Jesus taught the people that all people are to love and trust God as children do. The kingdom of God belongs to the children.

For more on the teachings of the Catholic Church on the kingdom of God, see *Catechism of the Catholic Church* paragraph numbers 541–550 and 2816–2821.

Sharing God's Word

Read together the Bible story in Mark 10:13–16 about Jesus blessing the children or you can read the adaptation of the story on page 191. Emphasize that Jesus invited the children to come to him and blessed them.

Praying

In this chapter your child prayed a prayer of meditation. This kind of prayer is also sometimes called guided imagery. Use the steps on page 195 and pray the prayer together.

Making a Difference

Choose one of the following activities to do as a family or design a similar activity of your own.

- Jesus taught us to love and trust God as children do. Talk about how your family shows that you love and trust God.

- Jesus welcomed everyone. He showed people that they are all loved by God. As a family, do one thing that will show people that they are loved by God.

- Discuss the ways your parish welcomes children. Name activities, events, and opportunities that are available for children in your parish.

For more ideas on ways your family can live your faith, visit the "Faith First for Families" page at **www.FaithFirst.com**. Click on "Games." Enjoy playing your child's games together.

A. The Best Word or Phrase

Complete the sentences. Color the circles next to the best choices.

1. Children of God are created to know, ____, and serve God.

   ○ love   ○ forgive

2. The Great ___ is to love God with our whole heart and to love others as we love ourselves.

   ○ Commandment   ○ Prayer

3. We show people ___ when we treat them as children of God.

   ○ respect   ○ fear

4. ___ hurt our friendship with God and with other people.

   ○ Good choices   ○ Sins

5. We need to ask for ___ when we have hurt someone.

   ○ forgiveness   ○ punishment

B. Words and Meanings

Match the two columns. Draw a line from the words in column A to their meanings in column B.

Column A

1. community

2. Moses

3. worship

Column B

a. A leader of God's people

b. Give praise and honor to God

c. People who care for one another

C. What I Learned

1. *What new thing did you learn about in this unit? Tell a partner.*

2. *Look at the list of faith words on page 132. Circle the ones that you know now.*

D. From a Scripture Story

Number the sentences in the order that they happened in the Bible story about Jesus and the children.

_____ Jesus said, "Let the children come to me."

_____ People brought their children to Jesus.

_____ The disciples told the people and the children to go away.

_____ Jesus blessed the children.

Where and when can we pray?

Getting Ready

What I Have Learned

What are some things you already know about prayer?

When to pray

_____

- -

_____

How to pray

_____

- -

_____

Where to pray

_____

- -

_____

Words to Know

Put an X next to the faith words you know. Put a ? next to the faith words you need to know more about.

Faith Words

_____ prayer

_____ trust

_____ psalms

_____ hymns

_____ Our Father

A Question I Have

What question would you like to ask about prayer?

_____

- -

_____

_____

- -

_____

From a Scripture Story

Jesus teaching his disciples to pray

What prayer did Jesus teach us to pray?

We Talk and Listen to God

We Pray

Lord God, hear our prayer. Amen.

What are some of our feelings?

We can feel happy or sad. We can feel glad or mad. We share with others what we are feeling. We can tell God what we are feeling too.

When do you tell God how you are feeling?

We Can Tell God Anything

Faith Focus

Why is it important to pray?

Faith Words

prayer
Prayer is listening and talking to God.

We Talk and Listen to God

Friends and families listen and talk to each other. We share what is on our minds and in our hearts.

Prayer is listening and talking to God. It is sharing with God what is on our minds and in our hearts. We can pray anywhere and anytime. The Holy Spirit helps us to pray. When we pray, we grow in our love for God.

 Learn to sign this message. Teach it to someone else.

 I

 talk

 to

 God.

Jesus Shows Us How to Pray

Jesus prayed all during his life. Sometimes Jesus prayed alone. Sometimes Jesus prayed with his family. Sometimes Jesus prayed with his friends. Sometimes Jesus prayed with his neighbors.

Sometimes we pray alone. Sometimes we pray with others. We pray with our family. We pray with our friends. We pray with our Church community.

Faith-Filled People

Thérèse The Little Flower

Saint Thérèse of Lisieux is also called the Little Flower. Thérèse found a favorite place to pray. When she was young, she would pray in the space between her bed and the wall. The Church celebrates the feast day of Saint Thérèse, the Little Flower, on October 1.

ACTIVITY *Circle your favorite place to pray. Why is it your favorite place?*

203

God Always Listens

Jesus told us that God is our Father. God the Father always listens to us. He wants us to share with him what is on our minds and in our hearts.

We do what Jesus taught us. We tell God the Father we love him. We thank him for his blessings. We ask God to take care of us and our family. We ask God to help other people. We ask God to forgive us and to help us to live as his children.

 Look at the pictures. Write a short prayer the child in one of the pictures might be saying.

God our loving Father,

_____

_____

_____

_____

_____

_____

Prayer Partners

The sixth graders at Nativity Parish wanted to help the first graders. They thought of many things to do. They chose to be their prayer partners.

The sixth graders sat with their prayer partners when they went to church. They helped the first graders to learn the words to the prayers and to sing the hymns. They taught them when to stand and when to sit and when to kneel.

As Jesus taught his disciples to pray, the sixth graders helped the first graders to pray.

QUESTION *Who helps you to learn how to pray? Tell that person "Thank you."*

Our Catholic Faith

Meal Prayers

We pray before and after meals. We ask God to bless us and the food we eat. We ask God to help people who do not have enough food.

What Difference Does Faith Make in My Life?

The Holy Spirit teaches you to pray.
You can talk to God about anything.
You can pray anywhere and anytime.

Fill in the chart. Name something or someone you can pray for at different times during the day.

Praying to God

Morning
_____
- -
_____

Afternoon
_____
- -
_____

Evening
_____
- -
_____

My Faith Choice

 This week I will pray in the morning,
afternoon, and evening.

Hail Mary

Mary, the mother of Jesus, teaches us to pray and prays for us. Learn these words from the Hail Mary. Pray them often. Pray them alone and with your family.

Hail Mary, full of grace,

the Lord is with thee.

Blessed art thou among women

and blessed is the fruit

of thy womb, Jesus.

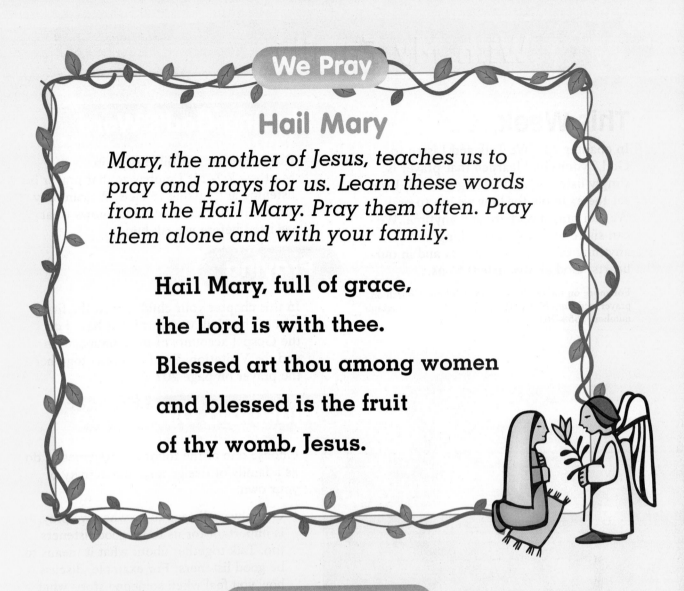

We Remember

Color the ◯ if the sentence is true.
Color the ▢ if the sentence is not true.

1. We can talk to God about anything. ◯ ▢

2. We can talk to God anywhere. ◯ ▢

3. We pray only by ourselves. ◯ ▢

To Help You Remember

1. Prayer is listening and talking to God.

2. When we pray, we grow in our love for God.

3. God always listens to our prayers.

This Week . . .

In chapter 23, "We Talk and Listen to God," your child learned that prayer is simply listening and talking to God. Jesus set the example for how we are to pray. We can pray anywhere and anytime. We can share with God everything and anything that is on our minds and in our hearts. God always listens to us.

For more on the teachings of the Catholic Church on prayer, see *Catechism of the Catholic Church*, paragraph numbers 2558–2619.

Sharing God's Word

Read together the Bible story in Matthew 7:7–11. Emphasize that prayer is listening and talking to God. We can pray anywhere and anytime. God knows what we need before we ask him.

Praying

In this chapter your child prayed the first part of the Hail Mary, which is based on the Gospel accounts of the Annunciation and the Visitation. Read and pray together the prayer on page 207.

Making a Difference

Choose one of the following activities to do as a family or design a similar activity of your own.

- God always listens to us when we pray. It is important for us to be good listeners too. Talk together about what it means to be good listeners. For example, discuss how you feel when someone stops what they are doing to listen to you, how good you are at listening to others, and so on.

- Go for a walk together. Thank God for everything you see and hear.

- Family prayer time helps us be aware that God is always with us. Evaluate your family prayer time. Do what it takes to integrate time for prayer into your family's daily activities and schedule.

For more ideas on ways your family can live your faith, visit the "Faith First for Families" page at **www.FaithFirst.com**. Click on "Bible Stories." Listening to Bible stories and thinking about them is a wonderful form of prayer.

Jesus Teaches His Followers to Pray

A Scripture Story

24

Jesus praying alone

We Pray

Lord Jesus, teach us to pray as you taught the disciples to pray. Amen.

What are your favorite prayers?

Sometimes we pray for ourselves. At other times we pray for our family and friends.

What are some prayers you pray with our Church family?

Bible Background

Faith Focus

What does Jesus teach us about praying?

Faith Words

trust

To trust someone is to believe that person will always do what is best for us.

Jesus Prayed

Jesus prayed for himself and for other people. He asked his Father to help him do the work his Father sent him to do. He asked God to forgive those who hurt him. Jesus asked God the Father to take care of his disciples.

Jesus prayed with his disciples and his neighbors. He listened to God's word with them. Jesus prayed with children when their parents brought them to him.

 Draw a picture of yourself praying with others.

Reading the Word of God

Jesus Teaches Us to Pray

Jesus taught his followers how to pray. One time Jesus was with his followers on a hillside. He said,

"You do not need to use many words when you talk to God. Talk to God from your heart."
Based on Matthew 6:7

God loves to hear our voice. We do not have to use many words. God always listens when we pray.

ACTIVITY *Close your eyes. Remember God is listening. Say a short prayer.*

Understanding the Word of God

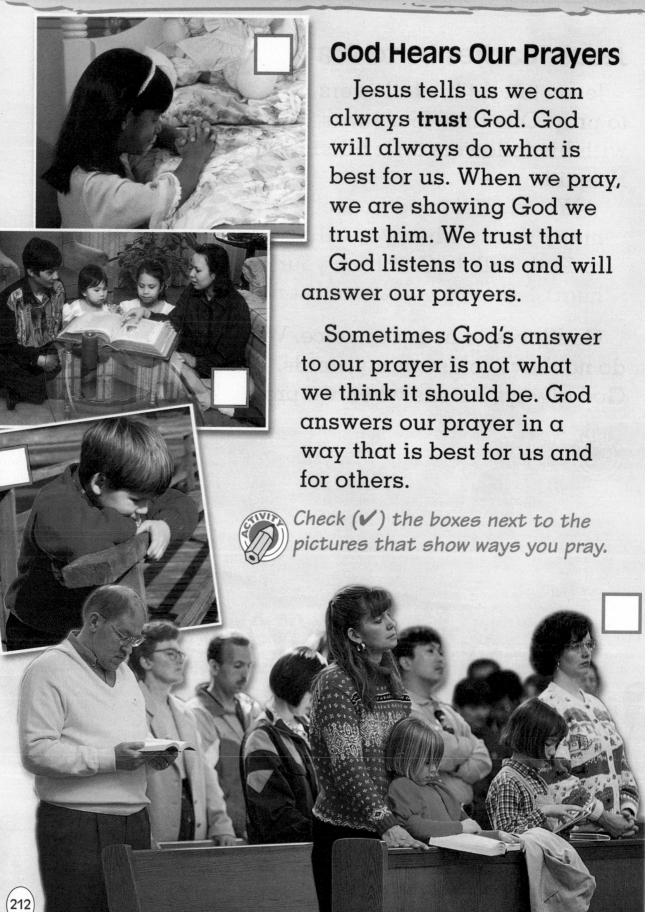

God Hears Our Prayers

Jesus tells us we can always **trust** God. God will always do what is best for us. When we pray, we are showing God we trust him. We trust that God listens to us and will answer our prayers.

Sometimes God's answer to our prayer is not what we think it should be. God answers our prayer in a way that is best for us and for others.

ACTIVITY Check (✔) the boxes next to the pictures that show ways you pray.

Our Church Makes a Difference

The Church Prays with the Community We Live In

In special times our Church joins with the community we live in to pray. We pray together in times of happiness and in times of sadness. We pray together to thank God for his blessings.

Our Church helps the community we live in to trust in God. Our Church asks God to help our community live in peace with one another and with other countries.

QUESTION *What prayer might the people in the picture be praying?*

REMEMBER OUR FIREFIGHTERS

What Difference Does Faith Make in My Life?

The Holy Spirit helps you to pray.
The Holy Spirit teaches you to pray.

Circle your favorite place to pray. Draw yourself praying in that place.

My Favorite Place to Pray

My Faith Choice

This week I will pray in the places that I have checked (✔).

❑ At home
❑ On the playground

❑ In church
❑ _____

A Simple Prayer

Our prayers can be very short. We can pray them many times throughout the day. Learn this prayer by heart. Pray the prayer often each day.

God, how great you are!

We Remember

Use the code to find out a message about prayer.

A	C	D	E	H	I	L
1	2	3	4	5	6	7

N	O	P	R	S	T	W	Y
8	9	10	11	12	13	14	15

___ ___   ___ ___ ___   ___ ___ ___ ___
14 4   2 1 8   10 11 1 15

___ ___ ___ ___ ___   ___ ___ ___
1 7 9 8 4   1 8 3

___ ___ ___ ___   ___ ___ ___ ___ ___ ___.
14 6 13 5   9 13 5 4 11 12

To Help You Remember

1. Jesus taught his followers to pray.

2. Jesus prayed alone and with others.

3. Jesus taught his disciples that God always answers our prayers in a way that is best for us and for others.

This Week . . .

In chapter 24, "Jesus Teaches His Followers to Pray: A Scripture Story," your child learned that Jesus taught us about prayer. Jesus taught that we do not need to use many words when we pray. God knows our heart; he knows what we will pray before we say a word. God always listens and answers our prayers in ways that are best for ourselves and for others. As Jesus did, we pray both alone and with others.

For more on the teachings of the Catholic Church on prayer, see *Catechism of the Catholic Church*, paragraph numbers 2650–2691.

Sharing God's Word

Read the Bible story in Matthew 6:5–8 about Jesus teaching his followers to pray or read the adaptation of the story on page 211. Emphasize that we do not need to use many words when we pray.

Praying

In this chapter your child prayed a simple five-word prayer. Read and pray together the prayer on page 215.

Making a Difference

Choose one of the following activities to do as a family or design a similar activity of your own.

- Sometimes Jesus went up on the mountaintop to pray. Invite each person to share where they feel close to God.

- The Mass is the most important prayer of the Church. When we participate in the celebration of Mass, it is important that we join with the assembly, pray the responses, and participate fully. Help one another and encourage one another to participate at Mass by praying the responses and singing the songs.

- Use the prayer on page 215 as your family prayer before meals this week.

For more ideas on ways your family can live your faith, visit the "Faith First for Families" page at **www.FaithFirst.com**. Click on "Gospel Reflections" and talk as a family about Sunday's Gospel reading.

We Pray in Many Ways

25

We Pray

God, we love you. We thank you for being so good to us.
                    Amen.

How do you share your thoughts and feelings?

We use words and actions to share our thoughts and feelings. We use words and actions to pray.

What is one way you pray using actions?

Praying to God

Faith Words

psalms
Psalms are prayer songs. The psalms the Church prays are found in the Bible.

hymns
Hymns are prayers we sing.

We Use Words to Pray

Words help us to share our thoughts and feelings. When we pray, we use words to share our thoughts and feelings with God.

Sometimes we join with others and pray aloud to God. Sometimes we speak quietly in our hearts to God.

 Pretend you are one of the children in this photo. What words or feelings are you sharing with God?

We Sing Our Prayers

One of the most beautiful ways we pray is by singing. We sing aloud for all to hear.

At Mass we sing **psalms** and **hymns.** Psalms and hymns are prayers we sing. Together we sing that we believe in God and love God with all our heart.

Use the code to finish this psalm prayer. Pray the psalm with your class and family.

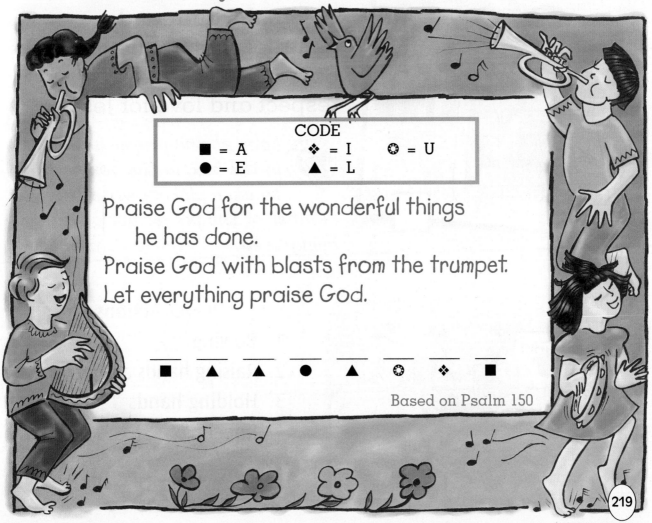

CODE

■ = A   ❖ = I   ✺ = U
● = E   ▲ = L

Praise God for the wonderful things
    he has done.
Praise God with blasts from the trumpet.
Let everything praise God.

■ ▲ ▲ ● ▲ ✺ ❖ ■

Based on Psalm 150

219

We Use Prayer Actions

Sometimes we use our hands when we pray. We fold our hands to show our love and respect for God. We use our right hand to bless ourselves when we pray the Sign of the Cross. Sometimes we hold each other's hands when we pray the Our Father.

We use other parts of our body too when we pray. We sit and stand. We bow before the altar and genuflect before the Blessed Sacrament. This shows respect and love for Jesus.

ACTIVITY *Look at the prayer actions in the box. In the box next to each picture write the number of the prayer action being used.*

Prayer Actions

1. Bowing
2. Raising hands and arms
3. Holding hands
4. Kneeling

Sacred Music

Sister Thea Bowman had a special gift from God. She had the gift of singing. Everywhere Sister Thea went she sang about God's love for everyone.

Sister Thea Bowman sang songs to praise God. She sang songs to help people share their love for God and for one another. She helped everyone to love and respect one another as children of God.

QUESTION? *What is your favorite song about God? Share the words of the song with a partner.*

Our Catholic Faith

Hymns

Hymns are songs we sing about our faith. We sing hymns about God the Father, about Jesus, and about the Holy Spirit. We sing hymns about Mary and the saints. We sing about God's love and forgiveness. Hymns we sing in church are found in a hymnal.

What Difference Does Faith Make in My Life?

You pray in many ways. You can use your arms, hands, body, and voice to pray.

Sing this prayer song to the tune of "Row, Row, Row Your Boat."

Sing to God

Sing, sing, sing a song.

Sing a song to God.

Praise God. Praise God.

Praise God. Praise God.

Sing a prayer to God.

My Faith Choice

This week I will pray to God each day. I will

_____

- -

_____.

Praying with Actions

We pray using words and actions. Pray a short prayer in your own words as you do each prayer action.

Dear God,

I pray to you with folded hands.
(Pray a silent prayer.)

I pray to you with a quiet voice.
(Pray a silent prayer.)

I pray to you as I stand.
(Pray aloud "Amen.")

We Remember

Draw lines from the words in Column A to the sentences in Column B that they complete.

Column A

a. hymns

b. genuflect

c. actions

Column B

1. We pray by using words and ___ .

2. We show our love for Jesus in the Blessed Sacrament when we ___ .

3. Prayers we sing are called ___ .

To Help You Remember

1. We can use our voices and bodies when we pray.

2. Our actions help us to pray.

3. We can pray by singing.

This Week . . .

In chapter 25, "We Pray in Many Ways," your child learned about the different ways we can pray. We not only use words, spoken aloud and in the quiet of our heart when we pray; we also use a variety of prayer actions, or gestures. We use our whole being to share our thoughts and feelings with God in prayer.

For more on the teachings of the Catholic Church on prayer, see *Catechism of the Catholic Church* paragraph numbers 1145–1158 and 2700–2719.

Sharing God's Word

Pray together Psalm 150. Pantomime the musical instruments named in the Psalm. Emphasize that we use all of creation to raise up our minds and hearts to God in prayer.

Praying

In this chapter your child prayed using both words and actions. Read and pray together the prayer on page 223.

Making a Difference

Choose one of the following activities to do as a family or design a similar activity of your own.

- Make up actions to accompany the praying of the prayer, "I love God." Pray the prayer often this week.

- We use words and actions when we pray. We pray quietly in our hearts and sing our prayers for all to hear. Choose a song that you can sing to God. Sing the song, using gestures to accompany the words.

- When you take part in the celebration of Mass this week, pay attention to all the gestures or actions. When you get home from church, try to name and write down all the actions that were used. Use appropriate gestures in your family prayer.

For more ideas on ways your family can live your faith, visit the "Faith First for Families" page at **www.FaithFirst.com**. Click on "Family Prayer." Use this week's prayer during your family prayer time this week.

Jesus Teaches Us the Our Father

A Scripture Story

26

We Pray

Our Father, who art in heaven, hallowed be thy name.

Amen.

Who has taught you to learn something new?

Many people help us to learn new things. Jesus taught the disciples to pray.

Who helps you learn to pray?

Bible Background

Faith Focus

What prayer did Jesus teach us to pray?

Faith Words

Our Father
The Our Father is the prayer Jesus taught his disciples.

Jesus Prayed

Jesus prayed often. He talked to God about everything. He listened to God.

The followers of Jesus were with Jesus when he prayed. They wanted to learn to pray as Jesus prayed.

 In each picture frame draw a picture of someone who has helped you to pray. Write the person's name under their picture.

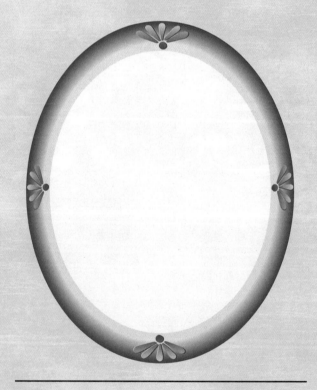

The Our Father

One day one of the disciples asked Jesus to teach them to pray. Jesus said,

"This is how you are to pray.
Our Father in heaven,
   hallowed be your name,
   your kingdom come,
   your will be done,
      on earth as in heaven.
   Give us today our daily bread;
   and forgive us our debts,
      as we forgive our debtors;
   and lead us not
      into temptation,
   but deliver us from evil."

Based on Matthew 6:9–13

Jesus taught the disciples to pray the **Our Father.** We also call the Our Father the Lord's Prayer.

ACTIVITY *Pretend you are one of the disciples in the picture. Pray the Our Father with Jesus.*

227

Jesus Teaches Us to Pray

When we pray the Our Father, we tell God that we believe he is our Father. We honor the name of God. We trust him with all our heart.

We ask God to help us to live as his children. We ask for forgiveness. We tell God that we forgive those who hurt us. We ask him to help us to do good and to live with him forever in heaven.

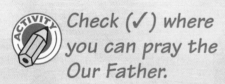 *Check (✓) where you can pray the Our Father.*

☐ At Mass

☐ At home

☐ On the school bus

☐ In the car

☐ In the park

Our Church Makes a Difference

Blessed Teresa of Calcutta

Mother Teresa of Calcutta took care of people who had no one else to take care of them. The people were very sick and very poor. They had no place to live.

Mother Teresa fed them. She washed them. Everything Mother Teresa did showed that God is everyone's Father. Everyone can pray, "Our Father." The Church honors Mother Teresa in a special way. The Church has named her Blessed Teresa of Calcutta.

QUESTION *What can you do to show that God is everyone's Father?*

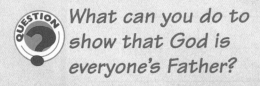

229

What Difference Does Faith Make in My Life?

When you pray the Our Father, you show that you believe that everyone is a child of God.

God Is Our Father

In the candle write a prayer to God your Father.

Dear God our Father,

_____
- -
_____
_____
- -
_____.

Your child,

_____
- -
_____

My Faith Choice

 I will choose to live as a child of God this week. Every day I will say the prayer that I wrote.

The Our Father

Every day Christians all around the world pray the Our Father. Pray the Our Father together.

**Our Father, who art in heaven,
hallowed be thy name;
thy kingdom come;
thy will be done on earth as it is in heaven.
Give us this day our daily bread;
and forgive us our trespasses
as we forgive those who trespass against us;
and lead us not into temptation,
but deliver us from evil. Amen.**

We Remember

Find and circle the words in the puzzle. Tell how each word reminds you that you are a child of God.

Jesus	Father
forgive	prayer

F O R G I V E T P
M C J E S U S W Z
O P R A Y E R K H
L P R F A T H E R

To Help You Remember

1. Jesus taught us to pray the Our Father.
2. The Our Father is a prayer for all God's children.
3. The Our Father is also called the Lord's Prayer.

This Week . . .

In chapter 26, "Jesus Teaches Us the Our Father: A Scripture Story," your child learned about praying the Our Father, or Lord's Prayer. Jesus not only gave the Our Father to his first disciples; he gave this wonderful prayer to all Christians of all times. Praying the Our Father teaches us to pray. It is a summary of the entire message of the Gospel.

For more on the teachings of the Catholic Church on the Our Father, see *Catechism of the Catholic Church* paragraph numbers 2759–2856.

Sharing God's Word

Read together the Bible story in Matthew 6:9–13 about Jesus teaching the disciples to pray the Our Father or read the adaptation of the story on page 227. Emphasize that praying the Our Father honors God and shows our trust in him.

Praying

In this chapter your child prayed the Our Father. Pray the Our Father with your child this week.

Making a Difference

Choose one of the following activities to do as a family or design a similar activity of your own.

- Practice saying the words of the Our Father with your child. When you take part in the celebration of Mass this week, help your child join in praying the Our Father with the assembly.

- Use the Our Father as your mealtime prayer this week. Remember that the Our Father is the prayer of all God's children. Christians pray the Our Father every day all around the world.

- Make an Our Father puzzle. Write the words of the Our Father on a piece of posterboard. Cut the posterboard into pieces. Put the puzzle together with your child. This will help your child learn the Our Father.

For more ideas on ways your family can live your faith, visit the "Faith First for Families" page at **www.FaithFirst.com**. "Gospel Reflections" will continue to change each week over the summer. Don't forget to visit this page often.

Name _____

A. The Best Word or Phrase

Complete the sentences. Color the circle next to the best choice for each sentence.

1. Prayer is listening and talking to ___.

   ○ **God**   ○ **our parents**

2. Jesus taught the disciples to pray the ___.

   ○ **Hail Mary**   ○ **Our Father**

3. We sing ___ and hymns at Mass.

   ○ **stories**   ○ **psalms**

4. We can fold our ___ when we pray.

   ○ **hands**   ○ **heart**

5. We use our right hand to bless ourselves when we pray the ___.

   ○ **Our Father**   ○ **Sign of the Cross**

B. Pray

Circle the number next to your favorite prayer. In the box draw yourself praying it in your favorite place.

1. The Sign of the Cross
2. The Our Father
3. The Glory Be
4. The Hail Mary
5. Psalm 150

C. What I Learned

1. What new thing have you learned about prayer in this unit? Tell your class.

2. Look at the list of faith words on page 200. Circle the ones that you know now.

D. From a Scripture Story

Jesus taught his disciples to pray the Our Father. Color the ☺ next to the words that tell us about the Our Father. Color the ☹ next to the words that do not tell us about the Our Father.

☺ ☹ We honor the name of God.

☺ ☹ We tell God we are afraid of him.

☺ ☹ We ask God to help us live as children of God.

☺ ☹ We promise to forgive people as God forgives us.

☺ ☹ We ask God to help us get to heaven.

How does the Church celebrate its faith all year long?

The Liturgical Year

The Church's year of prayer and worship is called the liturgical year. These are the seasons of the Church's year.

 Check (✔) your favorite season of the Church's year. Why is it your favorite season?

Advent

Advent begins the Church's year. We get our hearts ready to remember the birth of Jesus. The color for Advent is purple.

Christmas

At **Christmas** the Church celebrates the birth of Jesus, God's Son. The color for Christmas is white.

Lent

Lent is the time of the Church's year we remember Jesus died for us. It is a time to get ready for Easter. The color for Lent is purple.

Easter

During the **Easter** season we celebrate that Jesus was raised from the dead. Jesus gave us the gift of new life. The color for Easter is white.

Ordinary Time is the longest time of the Church's year. The color for Ordinary Time is green.

Ordinary Time

How does the Church celebrate our faith all year long?

Christmas

Lent and Easter

The Celebrations of Our Church

We decorate our classrooms all year long. Decorations remind us of the seasons of the year. They tell us about winter, spring, summer, and fall.

The Church has seasons too. We decorate our churches to celebrate these special times of the year. All year long we use different colors to help us celebrate.

The color we most often see is green. Green is the color for Ordinary Time. Ordinary Time is the longest time of the Church's year.

The seasons of the Church year are celebrated throughout the seasons of our year.

Ordinary Time

Advent

We Are Followers of Jesus

ACTIVITY During Ordinary Time we listen to the story of Jesus calling Peter, James, Andrew, and John to be his followers. Write or draw how you might live as a disciple of Jesus. Color the frame.

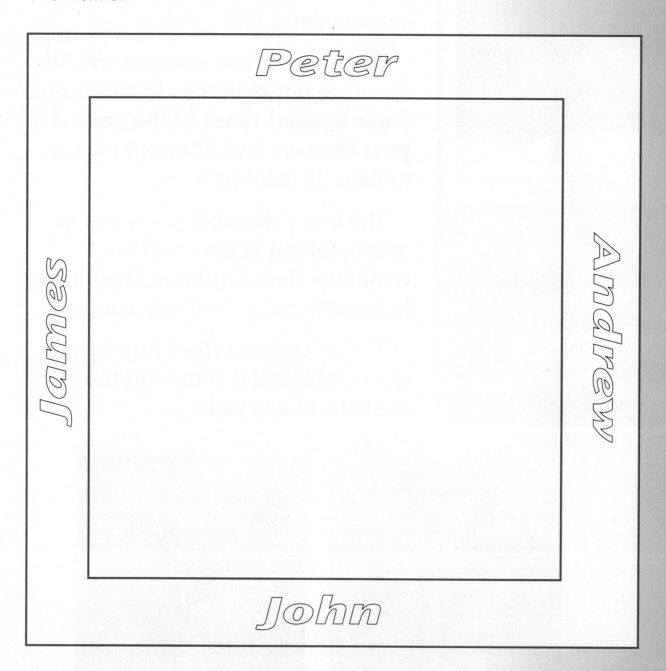

Peter

James

Andrew

John

The First Week of Advent

How does celebrating Advent help us to prepare for Christmas?

Jesus Is Our Light

The Church's season of Advent begins the Church's year. During Advent we prepare for Christmas. We light candles to chase away the winter darkness. These candles remind us that Jesus is the Light of the world.

Jesus asks us to be light for the world too. In Advent we let our light shine. We help people. We make gifts. We do secret good deeds for each other.

We gather in church and prepare our hearts to welcome Jesus. We sing and pray together. We remember that Jesus is with us every day.

My Light Shines

Decide what you can do to get ready for Christmas. Color in the flames to show what you will do.

I can help at home.

I can make a gift.

I can help a neighbor.

I can pray.

The Second Week of Advent

Who are we waiting for during Advent?

Get Ready!

Sometimes someone calls and announces, "Grandma is coming to visit you!" We get ourselves and our home ready for company.

John the Baptist announced the coming of Jesus. People crowded around him. They asked, "How can we get ready?" He told them to make room in their hearts for Jesus.

Many people changed their ways. When Jesus came, they welcomed him with gladness.

During Advent we listen to John's message. We make room in our hearts for Jesus. We turn from selfish ways. When Christmas comes, we want to be ready to welcome Jesus.

Prepare to Welcome Jesus

ACTIVITY *Color in the boxes that tell about children preparing their hearts for Jesus. Then make a choice to prepare your heart to welcome Jesus when Christmas comes.*

Henry feeds his gerbils every day.

Jose lets Angie ride his bike.

Kanisha prays for her grandma.

Susana pushes ahead of the others.

Patti will not do her chores.

Pablo watches over baby Dominic.

Maria keeps all the candy.

Jack laughs at Billy's mistake.

Faith Focus

How does the story of Mary visiting Elizabeth help us to get ready for Christmas?

Mary's Song

When we are happy, we sing for joy. We tell other people. Mary, the mother of Jesus, sang about her happiness. She also told someone.

The angel Gabriel came to Mary to ask her to be Jesus' mother. She said she would do whatever God asked. Then the angel told Mary that Elizabeth was going to have a baby too. Mary went to visit her.

Elizabeth saw Mary coming. She called Mary "blessed" because Mary said yes to God. Mary sang a prayer of praise and thanksgiving to God.

These two Gospel stories about Mary help us to get ready for Christmas. They teach us how to say yes to God.

An Advent Prayer

Pray this prayer together. Say yes to God as Mary did. Prepare your heart to get ready for Christmas.

Leader: Loving God, Christmas is almost here. Advent is almost over. Help us say yes with Mary. Amen.

Reader: *Read Luke 1:26–33, 38.*

Leader: God called Mary to be the mother of Jesus.

All: **And Mary said, "Yes."**

Leader: When God calls us,

All: **we will say, "Yes."**

Leader: When God asks us to help one another,

All: **we will say, "Yes."**

Leader: When God calls us to pray,

All: **we will say, "Yes."**

Leader: When God calls us today,

All: **we will say, "Yes."**

Leader: Let us pray together.

Child 1: Hail, Mary, full of grace, the Lord is with thee.

Child 2: Blessed art thou among women

Child 3: and blessed is the fruit of thy womb, Jesus.

All: **Holy Mary, Mother of God, pray for us sinners, now and at the hour of our death. Amen.**

The Fourth Week of Advent

Faith Focus

During Advent who have we been preparing to welcome?

All Is Ready

During Advent we wait. Long ago, God's people waited too. They waited for the new leader God promised would be born. They wanted him to care for them. He would care for God's people as a good shepherd cares for his sheep.

Micah the Prophet wrote that God's Promised One would be born in Bethlehem. Micah said, "He shall stand firm and shepherd his flock" (Micah 5:3).

The words of Micah came true. As Christmas draws near, we get ready to welcome Jesus our Savior who was born in Bethlehem. He is the Good Shepherd who watches over us.

Going to Bethlehem

 Follow the maze to help Mary and Joseph find Bethlehem. Say a prayer and welcome Jesus into your heart when you reach Bethlehem.

Christmas

Faith Focus

Why did the angels visit the shepherds?

The Birth of Jesus

We like good news. It makes us happy. On the night of Jesus' birth, some shepherds heard good news. Angels said to them,

"Today in Bethlehem the savior God promised to send you has been born."   Based on Luke 2:11

The shepherds hurried to Bethlehem. They found Jesus there lying in a manger, just as the angels said. The shepherds were Jesus' first visitors. They told others all that happened.

We want to welcome Jesus just as the shepherds did. We thank God for bringing joy that will never end. We tell others this good news.

Las Posadas

People in Mexico celebrate Las Posadas. They celebrate the journey of Mary and Joseph to the inn in Bethlehem. The words las posadas mean "the inn."

Mary and Joseph: In the name of God, can we stay here?

Innkeeper One: We have no room for you. We are too crowded!

Mary and Joseph: In the name of God, do you have room for us?

Innkeeper Two: We have no room here.

Mary and Joseph: In the name of God, do you have room for us?

Innkeeper Three: My inn is full. There is a stable in the hills. It is warm there against the chill.

Reader: *Read Luke 2:1–20.*

Leader: God our Father, we rejoice in the birth of your Son. May we always welcome him when he comes. May he be our joy now and forever. Amen.

Epiphany

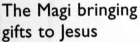

Faith Focus

What do we celebrate on Epiphany?

The Savior of the World

During Advent we waited and prepared for Christmas. We waited and prepared to welcome Jesus, the Son of God.

Today we hear the story of the Magi. They traveled a long distance to find Jesus. They went to Bethlehem and honored Jesus.

We want the whole world to celebrate the birth of the newborn Savior. We want heaven and nature to sing and rejoice. Jesus is the Savior of the world.

The Magi bringing gifts to Jesus

We Announce the Birth of the Savior of the World

 Make the cover for a Christmas card. Draw a picture and use words. Tell everyone that Jesus is the Savior of the world.

The First Week of Lent

How does celebrating Lent help us to get ready for Easter?

A Time to Grow

Think about spring. Remember how plants push their way up through the earth. Trees sprout leaves and buds. Birds sing their best songs.

In spring we plant new seeds. We cut away dead twigs and stems. We prepare for new life.

Jesus talked about death and new life. He held up a seed and said,

"I say to you, unless a grain of wheat falls to the ground and dies, it remains just a grain of wheat; but if it dies, it produces much fruit." John 12:24

During Lent we clear a place to plant seeds of faith and love. We work and pray. We grow in faith and love.

251

New Life

ACTIVITY Put this picture story in order. Number the pictures from 1 to 6. Share the story with a friend. Tell how the story helps us to understand Lent.

Praying Time

We like to talk with our friends. God is a friend who is always near. We talk with God in prayer.

Jesus taught that we are to pray every day. He says that God hears our prayers. God gives us all that is good for us.

Lent is a special time for prayer. It is a good time to offer praise and thanks. It is a good time to tell God our needs each and every day.

Lent is also a good time to join others in prayer. On Sunday we come together in our parish church. We praise and thank God together. We especially give thanks for Jesus.

My Prayer

Dear God,

I praise and thank you for

and

.

I ask you to watch over

and

.

Keep them in your care.

Amen.

254

The Third Week of Lent

Faith Focus

How does celebrating Lent help us to grow as followers of Jesus?

Better and Better

Making good choices helps us to grow as children of God. Once Jesus invited a tax collector to make a choice to be a follower of Jesus. The tax collector made the choice to leave his work and follow Jesus. The man's name was Matthew. He became one of Jesus' first disciples.

Jesus asks us to follow him too. During Lent we take special care to do the things Jesus asks us to do. We forgive. We find ways to make peace. We give to others who are in need. We ask God to help us to make everything just a little bit better.

A Helping Prayer

Jesus taught us to treat one another as he treated people. Pray this prayer this Lent.

Leader: When we can share
by opening a door,

All: **Lord, every little bit helps.**

Leader: When we can help
by sweeping the floor,

All: **Lord, every little bit helps.**

Leader: When we can add
to the family fun,

All: **Lord, every little bit helps.**

Leader: When it won't work
with just one,

All: **Lord, every little bit helps.**

Leader: When we need to pitch in to
care for a pet,

All: **Lord, every little bit helps.**

Leader: When sharing is needed,
don't let me forget,

All: **Lord, every little bit helps.**
Lord, help us today.
Amen.

Giving Our Time

We all like to help others. We like others to help us too.

Jesus asks us to help quietly. He tells us not to toot a loud horn so that everyone notices us doing good. Jesus says that only God needs to know our actions.

Jesus shows us many ways to give our time to help others. We can visit people who are alone. We can feed people who are hungry.

Lent is a giving time. We give our time. We share what we own. We work together to care for those in need. We pray for everyone who needs God's help and care.

We Share Our Time

 We can help others as Jesus asked us to do. Write what you can do at different times of the day. Ask the Holy Spirit to help you to do the things you wrote.

In the morning I can

_____

- .

During the day I can

_____

- .

After school I can

_____

- .

At night I can

_____

- .

Faith Focus

How can we grow as people who forgive others as God forgives us?

The Gift of Forgiveness

Has anyone ever said something that hurt you? Can you remember a time when it was hard to forgive?

Jesus says that all his followers must be ready to forgive. We are not only to forgive someone one time but over and over again.

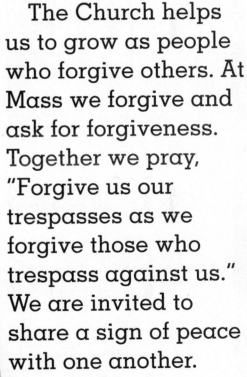

The Church helps us to grow as people who forgive others. At Mass we forgive and ask for forgiveness. Together we pray, "Forgive us our trespasses as we forgive those who trespass against us." We are invited to share a sign of peace with one another.

During Lent we remember that God forgives us over and over. We try to become forgiving people.

Forgive Always

Use the code to find out what Jesus teaches about forgiveness. Think about how you can live what Jesus tells us to do.

A	D	E	F	G	H	I
1	2	3	4	5	6	7

N	O	R	T	U	V
8	9	10	11	12	13

"$\frac{\text{F}}{4}$ $\frac{\text{O}}{9}$ $\frac{\text{R}}{10}$ $\frac{\text{G}}{5}$ $\frac{\text{I}}{7}$ $\frac{\text{V}}{13}$ $\frac{\text{E}}{3}$ $\frac{\text{O}}{9}$ $\frac{\text{N}}{8}$ $\frac{\text{E}}{3}$

$\frac{\text{A}}{1}$ $\frac{\text{N}}{8}$ $\frac{\text{O}}{9}$ $\frac{\text{T}}{11}$ $\frac{\text{H}}{6}$ $\frac{\text{E}}{3}$ $\frac{\text{R}}{10}$ $\frac{\text{O}}{9}$ $\frac{\text{V}}{13}$ $\frac{\text{E}}{3}$ $\frac{\text{R}}{10}$

$\frac{\text{A}}{1}$ $\frac{\text{N}}{8}$ $\frac{\text{D}}{2}$ $\frac{\text{O}}{9}$ $\frac{\text{V}}{13}$ $\frac{\text{E}}{3}$ $\frac{\text{R}}{10}$

$\frac{\text{A}}{1}$ $\frac{\text{G}}{5}$ $\frac{\text{A}}{1}$ $\frac{\text{I}}{7}$ $\frac{\text{N}}{8}$."

Based on Matthew 18:22

Palm Sunday of the Lord's Passion

Faith Focus

How do we begin our celebration of Holy Week?

Welcoming Jesus

Sometimes important people come to our town or school. We go out and greet them. We cheer and rejoice!

Once Jesus came to the city of Jerusalem. When Jesus came to the city, the people cheered. They waved branches from palm trees. They also spread their cloaks on the road to honor Jesus.

We remember this event at the beginning of Holy Week on Palm Sunday of the Lord's Passion. On this day we carry palm branches and honor Jesus too.

Honoring Jesus

These words are hidden in the puzzle. Find and circle the words. Use the words to tell a partner about Palm Sunday.

Jesus   **cloak**   **Jerusalem**   **Holy Week**   **palms**

T H O L Y W E E K E
P A L M S P C R L K
G J E R U S A L E M
L F M C L O A K B K
S E D M J E S U S T

Jesus and the disciples at the Last Supper

Faith Focus

What does the Church celebrate on Holy Thursday?

The Gift of the Eucharist

Holy Thursday is one of the most important days for our Church. On this day we remember and celebrate the day on which Jesus gave us the Eucharist.

On the night before he died, Jesus celebrated a special meal with his disciples. We call this meal the Last Supper. At the Last Supper Jesus took bread and said to the disciples, "This is my body." He also took a cup of wine and said, "This is the cup of my blood." Then Jesus said to them, "Do this in memory of me" (based on Luke 22:14–19).

We celebrate the Eucharist every time we celebrate Mass. When we do, we are doing what Jesus asked.

Thank You, Jesus!

 Use the code to color the stained-glass window. Use the stained-glass window to tell what happened at the Last Supper.

1 yellow

2 blue

3 purple

4 green

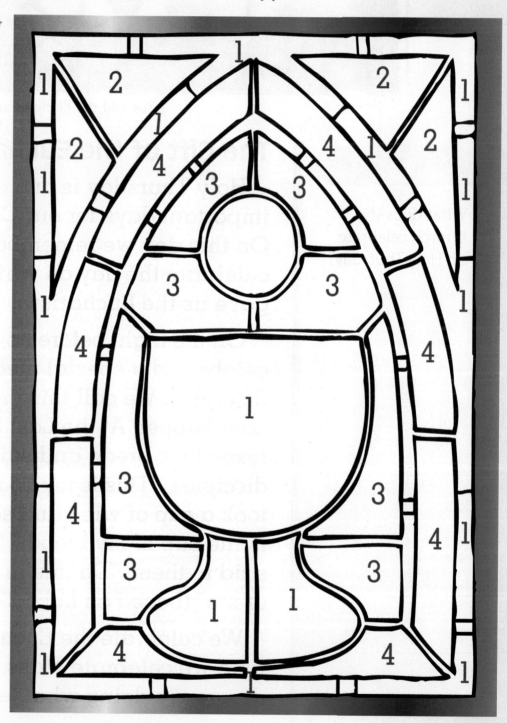

The Cross of Jesus

Sometimes we look at pictures or a gift that someone has given us. This helps us to remember and think about that person. What do you look at to help you remember someone?

The Friday of Holy Week is called Good Friday. It is the day we remember in a special way that Jesus suffered and died for us. On Good Friday the deacon or priest holds up a cross for us to look at. Looking at the cross, we think about and remember how much Jesus loves us. One way we show our love for Jesus is by loving one another.

Showing Our Love for Others

ACTIVITY *Color the ✝ next to the ways you can show your love for others. Show your love by doing the things you can do.*

✝ Help a friend who is sad.

✝ Forgive someone.

✝ Talk back to my parents.

✝ Do my chores cheerfully.

✝ _____

_____

Easter People

At Easter we see signs of new life all around us. These signs remind us that Jesus was raised from the dead to new life. We call this the Resurrection of Jesus. On Easter Sunday Christians celebrate Jesus' Resurrection.

Christians are Easter people! Alleluia is our song! We sing Alleluia over and over during the fifty days of the Easter season. The word *Alleluia* means "Praise the Lord!" We praise God for raising Jesus from the dead to new life.

Every Sunday in the year is a little Easter. We sing. We rest. We enjoy one another. All year long we praise and thank God.

Praise the Lord

ACTIVITY

Decorate the Easter banner. Use colors and words about new life. Show your finished banner to your friends and your family. Tell them about the Resurrection of Jesus.

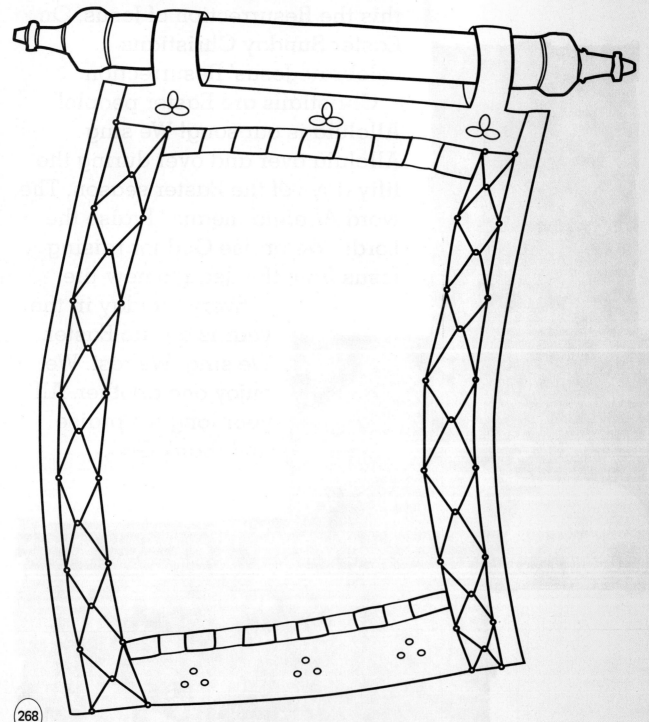

The Second Week of Easter

Faith Focus

Who are some of the disciples who saw the Risen Jesus?

Sharing the Good News

We hear good news. Then we proclaim, or announce, it to others. During the Easter season we announce, "Christ is risen!" For seven Sundays the Church joyfully tells Easter stories.

During Easter we hear about the people who first saw the Risen Jesus. We hear about Mary Magdalene, who saw the Risen Jesus and announced, "I have seen the Lord" (John 20:18). We hear about two other disciples who knew the Risen Jesus in the breaking of the bread. We hear that when Thomas the Apostle saw the Risen Jesus, he said, "My Lord and my God!" (John 20:28).

We believe in the Risen Lord. We show others that we believe in Jesus by what we say and do.

Jesus Is Risen

ACTIVITY *Use your favorite colors to fill in the squares that show the ways you can be a good follower of Jesus.*

I can help out around
the house. ☐

I can say my prayers each day. ☐

I can pay better attention
in school. ☐

I can play with someone who
has no one to play with. ☐

I can make a card to cheer
someone up. ☐

I can remember that God
always loves me. ☐

Faith Focus

What do we mean when we say that Jesus is the vine and we are the branches?

One with Jesus

How do you feel when someone calls you their friend? One day Jesus called his disciples his friends. He said, "You are my friends" (John 15:14).

Jesus wanted the disciples to know how special his friendship with them was. He was as close to them as a vine is to its branches. This is how he talked about their friendship. He said,

"I am the vine, you are the branches." John 15:5

After Jesus died and was raised to new life, the disciples understood how much Jesus loved them. They knew how close they were to Jesus. They were one with him as a vine and its branches are one.

Jesus is one with us. He makes us one. At Easter we celebrate that we are one with the Risen Lord.

"I am the vine, you are the branches."

Alive in the Lord

ACTIVITY *Print your name on one branch. Print the names of your parents, a priest, and other people of the Church on the other branches. Share how the story of the vine and branches tells you about Jesus and the Church.*

Christ Is Risen

When someone loves us, we feel happy. Our smiling faces and actions tell people that we are lovable and loving and loved.

Out of love, God raised Jesus to new life. Jesus told his disciples to proclaim this Good News to everyone. Then the Risen Jesus returned to his Father.

The disciples were filled with joy and hope. They knew that God loved them. The disciples told everyone the good news about Jesus. We tell others about the Risen Lord by our words and actions.

Every Sunday

At Mass we show we believe in the Risen Jesus.
Trace the dots to discover the missing words.
Say the prayer aloud to tell others you believe
that Jesus rose from the dead to new life.

We proclaim your __Death__ ,

O Lord, and profess your

__Resurrection__

until __you__

__come__ again.

Faith Focus

How did the early Christians show their love for one another?

The Church Grows

Each Sunday during the Easter season, we hear stories from the Acts of the Apostles. This book of the New Testament tells us about how people became followers of Jesus.

Jesus' followers loved one another as Jesus asked them to do. They offered food and clothing to people who needed them. They made sure everyone had a place to live. They prayed for one another. They took care of those who were sick.

Many other people became Jesus' followers when they saw what the first Christians were doing. They wanted to do the loving things Jesus taught his disciples to do.

Following Jesus

 Use the words in the box and the sentence clues to complete this puzzle.

Easter   Bible   prayed   followers   loved   Jesus

DOWN

1. Jesus loved his f ___ .
3. Jesus' followers l ____ one another.
4. We show that we love J____ by our words and actions.

ACROSS

2. The Acts of the Apostles is a book in the B____.
5. During E____ we hear stories about how the Church grew.
6. The followers of Jesus p____ for one another.

Write one way you can show your love for others.

_____

_____

Why do we say that Jesus is our Good Shepherd?

The Good Shepherd

Some of us have read stories about shepherds. Some of us have seen sheep on hillsides out in the country. At Mass during the Easter season we hear Jesus tell us that he is the Good Shepherd and we are his sheep. Once Jesus told Peter the Apostle to lead and take care of the Church. He said to Peter,

"Feed my lambs" and "Feed my sheep."

John 21:15, 17

Jesus asked Peter to be a good shepherd to all of us.

Jesus is our Good Shepherd. A good shepherd is willing to give his life for his sheep. During Easter we remember Jesus' love for us.

Jesus the Good Shepherd

A Shepherd's Care

 Read these Bible passages about
the work and care of the Good Shepherd.

The Lord is my ;

to safe

you lead me.

You guide me along the right  .

Based on Psalm 23:1, 2, 3

Like a

he feeds his  ;

in his arms he gathers the .

Based on Isaiah 40:11

There will be one ,

one .

Based on John 10:16

Jesus Returns to His Father

Forty days after Easter, the Risen Jesus led his disciples outside Jerusalem. He reminded them that he had suffered, died, and was raised to new life. Jesus said that they should share this Good News with everyone. Jesus blessed them and returned to his Father in heaven.

The Church celebrates the day the Risen Jesus returned to his Father. We call this day the feast of the Ascension.

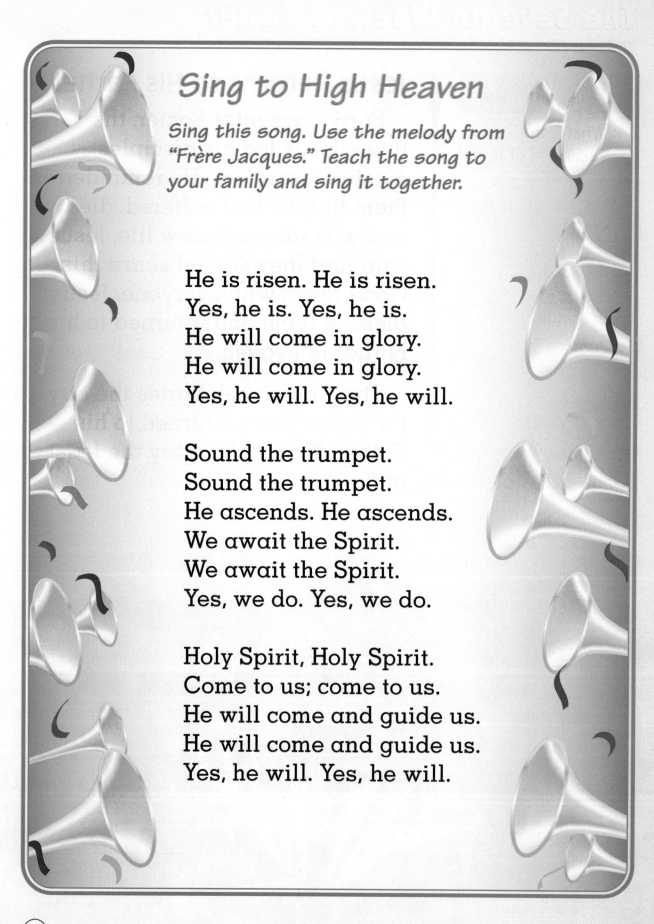

Sing to High Heaven

Sing this song. Use the melody from "Frère Jacques." Teach the song to your family and sing it together.

He is risen. He is risen.
Yes, he is. Yes, he is.
He will come in glory.
He will come in glory.
Yes, he will. Yes, he will.

Sound the trumpet.
Sound the trumpet.
He ascends. He ascends.
We await the Spirit.
We await the Spirit.
Yes, we do. Yes, we do.

Holy Spirit, Holy Spirit.
Come to us; come to us.
He will come and guide us.
He will come and guide us.
Yes, he will. Yes, he will.

Faith Focus

When does the Holy Spirit help us to live as followers of Jesus?

The Gift of the Holy Spirit

Sometimes we receive a gift that we use to help others. We have received that kind of gift from Jesus.

After Jesus returned to his Father, the disciples received the gift of the Holy Spirit. The Holy Spirit helped them to share the Good News about Jesus with others. The Holy Spirit helped them to do good work in Jesus' name.

On Pentecost we remember that the Holy Spirit came to the disciples. We too have received the gift of the Holy Spirit. The Holy Spirit helps us to do good. When we do good things in Jesus' name, we lead others to Jesus.

The Gift of the Holy Spirit

Work with a partner and follow this maze.
At each place stop to share the Good News
about Jesus with each other.

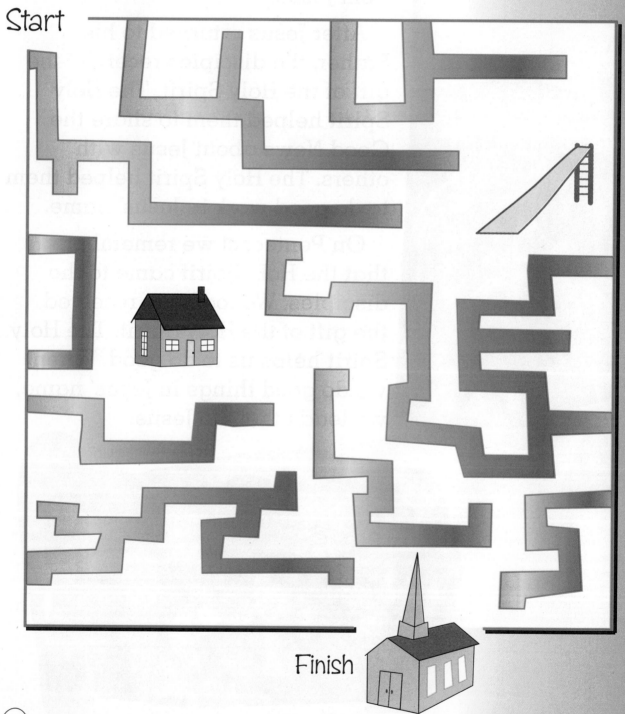

Start

Finish

Catholic Prayers and Practices

Sign of the Cross

In the name of the Father,
and of the Son,
and of the Holy Spirit. Amen.

Lord's Prayer

Our Father, who art in heaven,
hallowed be thy name;
thy kingdom come,
thy will be done
     on earth as it is in heaven.
Give us this day our daily bread,
and forgive us our trespasses,
as we forgive those who trespass
     against us;
and lead us not into temptation,
but deliver us from evil.
Amen.

Glory Be

Glory be to the Father
and to the Son
and to the Holy Spirit,
as it was in the beginning
is now, and ever shall be
world without end. Amen.

Hail Mary

Hail, Mary, full of grace,
the Lord is with thee.
Blessed art thou among women
and blessed is the fruit of thy
     womb, Jesus.
Holy Mary, Mother of God,
pray for us sinners,
now and at the hour of our death.
Amen.

Act of Contrition

My God,
I am sorry for my sins
     with all my heart.
In choosing to do wrong
and failing to do good,
I have sinned against you
whom I should love above all things.
I firmly intend, with your help,
to do penance,
to sin no more,
and to avoid whatever leads me to sin.
Our Savior Jesus Christ
suffered and died for us.
In his name, my God, have mercy.

Apostles' Creed

I believe in God,
the Father almighty,
Creator of heaven and earth,
and in Jesus Christ,
   his only Son, our Lord,

*(At the words that follow, up to and
including* the Virgin Mary, *all bow.)*

who was conceived by the Holy Spirit,
born of the Virgin Mary,
suffered under Pontius Pilate,
was crucified, died and was buried;
he descended into hell;
on the third day he rose again
   from the dead;
he ascended into heaven,
and is seated at the right hand
   of God the Father almighty;
from there he will come to judge
   the living and the dead.

I believe in the Holy Spirit,
the holy catholic Church,
the communion of saints,
the forgiveness of sins,
the resurrection of the body,
and life everlasting. Amen.

Nicene Creed

I believe in one God,
the Father almighty,
maker of heaven and earth,
of all things visible and invisible.

I believe in one Lord Jesus Christ,
the Only Begotten Son of God,
born of the Father before all ages.
God from God, Light from Light,
true God from true God,
begotten, not made, consubstantial
   with the Father;
through him all things were made.
For us men and for our salvation
he came down from heaven,

*(At the words that follow, up to and
including* and became man, *all bow.)*

and by the Holy Spirit
   was incarnate of the Virgin Mary,
and became man.

For our sake he was crucified under
   Pontius Pilate,
he suffered death and was buried,
and rose again on the third day
in accordance with the Scriptures.
He ascended into heaven
and is seated at the right hand
   of the Father.
He will come again in glory
to judge the living and the dead
and his kingdom will have no end.

I believe in the Holy Spirit, the Lord,
   the giver of life,
who proceeds from the Father and the Son,
who with the Father and the Son
   is adored and glorified,
who has spoken through the prophets.

I believe in one, holy, catholic and
   apostolic Church.
I confess one Baptism
   for the forgiveness of sins
and I look forward to the resurrection
   of the dead
and the life of the world to come.
Amen.

Morning Prayer

Dear God,
as I begin this day,
keep me in your love and care.
Help me to live as your child today.
Bless me, my family, and my friends
    in all we do.
Keep us all close to you. Amen.

Evening Prayer

Dear God,
I thank you for today.
Keep me safe throughout the night.
Thank you for all the good I did today.
I am sorry for what I have chosen
    to do wrong.
Bless my family and friends. Amen.

Grace Before Meals

Bless us, O Lord,
    and these thy gifts,
which we are about to receive
    from thy bounty,
through Christ our Lord.
Amen.

Grace After Meals

We give thee thanks, for all
    thy benefits, almighty God,
who lives and reigns forever.
Amen.

A Vocation Prayer

God, I know you will call me
for special work in my life.
Help me follow Jesus each day
and be ready to answer your call.

Rosary

Catholics pray the Rosary to honor Mary and remember the important events in the life of Jesus and Mary. There are twenty mysteries of the Rosary. Follow the steps from 1 to 5.

3. Think of the first mystery. Pray an Our Father, 10 Hail Marys, and the Glory Be.

5. Pray the Hail, Holy Queen prayer. Make the Sign of the Cross.

2. Pray an Our Father, 3 Hail Marys, and the Glory Be.

4. Repeat step 3 for each of the next 4 mysteries.

1. Make the Sign of the Cross and pray the Apostles' Creed.

Joyful Mysteries

1. The Annunciation
2. The Visitation
3. The Nativity
4. The Presentation in the Temple
5. The Finding of the Child Jesus After Three Days in the Temple

Luminous Mysteries

1. The Baptism at the Jordan
2. The Miracle at Cana
3. The Proclamation of the Kingdom and the Call to Conversion
4. The Transfiguration
5. The Institution of the Eucharist

Sorrowful Mysteries

1. The Agony in the Garden
2. The Scourging at the Pillar
3. The Crowning with Thorns
4. The Carrying of the Cross
5. The Crucifixion and Death

Glorious Mysteries

1. The Resurrection
2. The Ascension
3. The Descent of the Holy Spirit at Pentecost
4. The Assumption of Mary
5. The Crowning of the Blessed Virgin as Queen of Heaven and Earth

Hail, Holy Queen

Hail, holy Queen, Mother of mercy:
Hail, our life, our sweetness and our hope.
To you do we cry, poor banished
    children of Eve.
To you do we send up our sighs,
mourning and weeping
    in this valley of tears.
Turn then, most gracious advocate,
your eyes of mercy toward us;
and after this our exile
show unto us the blessed fruit
    of your womb, Jesus.
O clement, O loving, O sweet Virgin Mary.

The Great Commandment

"You shall love the Lord, your God, with all your heart, with all your soul, and with all your mind. . . . You shall love your neighbor as yourself."

Matthew 22:37, 39

Jesus' Commandment

"This is my commandment: love one another as I love you."

John 15:12

The Ten Commandments

1. I am the LORD your God: you shall not have strange Gods before me.
2. You shall not take the name of the LORD your God in vain.
3. Remember to keep holy the LORD's Day.
4. Honor your father and your mother.
5. You shall not kill.
6. You shall not commit adultery.
7. You shall not steal.
8. You shall not bear false witness against your neighbor.
9. You shall not covet your neighbor's wife.
10. You shall not covet your neighbor's goods.

Based on Exodus 20:2–3, 7–17

The Seven Sacraments

Jesus gave the Church a special way to worship God. He gave us the seven sacraments. The sacraments are celebrations of the Church. They are signs of God's love for us. When we celebrate the sacraments, Jesus is really present with us in a special way.

Anointing of the Sick

We receive God's healing strength when we are sick or dying.

Baptism

We become members of the Church and followers of Jesus.

Confirmation

We receive the Holy Spirit who helps us to live as children of God.

Holy Orders

A man is called by God to serve the Church as a bishop, priest, or deacon.

Eucharist

We receive the Body and Blood of Jesus.

Penance and Reconciliation

We celebrate God's gift of forgiveness and peace.

Matrimony

A man and a woman make a lifelong promise to love and respect each other.

We Celebrate the Mass

The Introductory Rites

We remember that we are the community
of the Church. We prepare to listen to the readings
from the Bible and to celebrate the Eucharist.

We stand and sing a song
as the priest and other
ministers go to the altar.
The priest greets us and
leads us in praying the
Sign of the Cross. We
admit our wrongdoings
and bless God for his
mercy. The priest leads us
in prayer.

The Liturgy of the Word

God speaks to us today.
We listen and respond to God's word.

At Mass on Sunday we
sit and listen to three
readings from the Bible.
After the first two readings
we respond, **"Thanks be to
God."** Then we stand and
listen as the deacon or
priest reads the Gospel.
We respond, **"Praise to
you, Lord Jesus Christ."**

The Liturgy of the Eucharist

**We join with Jesus and the Holy Spirit
to give thanks and praise to God the Father.**

Preparation of the Gifts

We bring the gifts of bread and wine to the altar. The priest offers our gifts of bread and wine to God. We respond, **"Blessed be God for ever."**

The Eucharistic Prayer

The priest invites us to join in praying a prayer of praise and thanksgiving to God the Father. Our gifts of bread and wine become the Body and Blood of Christ.

Communion Rite

We prepare our minds and hearts to receive the Body and Blood of Christ. We stand and pray the Lord's Prayer together. Then we share a sign of peace. We receive the Body and Blood of Christ in Holy Communion.

The Concluding Rites

We are sent forth to do good works, praising and blessing the Lord.

We stand as the priest blesses us in the name of the Father, and of the Son, and of the Holy Spirit. We sing a hymn as the priest, deacon, and the other ministers leave in procession. We go forth to love and serve God and others.

A Tour of a Church

Some churches are made of stone and some are wooden. Some are big and some are small. One thing churches all have in common is that they are places where people worship God.

Baptismal Font

The baptismal font is the pool of water used for Baptism. Water is used to remind us of new life. The tall candle is called the Easter candle. It is lit during Baptism to remind us of Jesus, the Light of the world.

Assembly

The assembly is the people gathered for Mass. The pews are the seats where the people sit.

Crucifix

The crucifix is a sign of Jesus' love for us. You see the crucifix near the altar. Not all crucifixes are the same. This one shows Jesus after he was raised from the dead. The crucifix reminds us that Jesus died and was raised again to new life.

Altar

The altar is the table where the Liturgy of the Eucharist is celebrated at Mass. It reminds us of the Last Supper and that Jesus died for us. The altar is also called the Table of the Lord. It is the table from which Jesus shares his Body and Blood with us.

Ambo

The ambo is the special stand or place from where the Scriptures are read during Mass. The lector is the person who reads the first and second readings during Mass. The deacon or priest reads the Gospel.

Book of the Gospels
Lectionary

The Book of the Gospels contains the Gospel readings we listen to at Mass. The first two readings are read from the Lectionary.

Tabernacle

The tabernacle is where the Eucharist, or Blessed Sacrament, is kept. When the candle next to the tabernacle is lit, it means that the Blessed Sacrament is in the tabernacle.

Glossary

Advent
[page 90]

_____ is the first season of the Church's year. We prepare for Christmas and get our hearts ready for Jesus.

Angels
[page 38]

_____ give honor and glory to God. They are God's messengers and helpers.

Baptism
[page 98]

_____ is the first sacrament we celebrate. In Baptism we receive the gift of God's life and become members of the Church.

Believe
[page 14]

_____ means to have faith in God. It means to give ourselves to God with all our heart.

Bible
[page 38]

The _____ is the written word of God. It is God's very own word to us.

Catholic
[page 70]

A _____ is a follower of Jesus who is a member of the Catholic Church.

children of God
[page 134]

All people are

_____

- -

_____ .

God created all people in his image.

- -

Christians
[page 78]

_____ are followers
of Jesus Christ. They believe in Jesus Christ and
live as he taught.

- -

Christmas
[page 91]

_____ comes after
Advent. It is the time of the Church's year when
we remember and celebrate the birth of Jesus.

- -

Church
[page 70]

The _____ is the People
of God who believe in Jesus and live as his
followers.

- -

Church's year
[page 90]

The _____
is made up of five seasons. They are Advent,
Christmas, Lent, Easter, and Ordinary Time.

- -

community
[page 150]

A _____ is a group
of people who respect and care for one another.

Creator
[page 22]

God is the _____. God made everything out of love and without any help.

cross
[page 46]

The _____ is a sign of our faith in Jesus. It reminds us that Jesus died on a cross so we could live forever in heaven.

Crucifixion
[page 46]

The _____ of Jesus is Jesus being put to death on a cross.

Disciples
[page 46]

_____ are followers of Jesus.

Easter
[page 90]

_____ is the season of the Church's year when we celebrate that Jesus was raised from the dead.

Eucharist
[page 114]

The _____ is the sacrament in which we receive the Body and Blood of Christ.

Faith
[page14]

_____ is a gift from God. It helps us to know God and to believe in God.

Galilee
[page 122]

_____ was one of the main places where Jesus taught and helped people.

God the Father
[pages 24 and 62]

_____ knows and loves us. God the Father is the first Person of the Holy Trinity.

Glory
[page 134]

_____ is another word for praise.

Gospel
[page 106]

The _____ is the Good News that Jesus told us about God's love.

Great Commandment
[page 150]

The _____ is to love God above all else and to love others as we love ourselves.

Heaven
[page 46]

_____ is living with God forever after we die.

Holy Family
[page 30]

The _____ is the family of Jesus, Mary, and Joseph.

Holy Spirit
[page 62]

The _____ is the third Person of the Holy Trinity. The Holy Spirit is always with us to be our helper.

Holy Trinity
[page 62]

The _____ is one God in three Persons—God the Father, God the Son, and God the Holy Spirit.

honor
[page 174]

We _____ people when we treat them with great respect.

Hymns
[page 218]

_____ are prayers we sing.

image of God
[page 22]

We are created in the _____. We are children of God.

Jesus
[page 30]

_____ is the Son of God. Jesus is truly God and truly man.

kingdom of God
[page 190]

The _____ is the kingdom of heaven.

Last Supper
[page 116]

The _____ is the meal Jesus ate with his disciples on the night before he died.

Lent
[page 92]

_____ is the time of the Church's year when we remember that Jesus died for us. We get ready for Easter.

Lord's Prayer
[page 229]

The _____ is another name for the Our Father.

Mary
[page 31]

_____ is the mother of Jesus, the Son of God.

Mass
[page 114]

The _____ is the most important celebration of the Church.

marriage
[page 142]

A _____ is the lifelong promise made by a man and a woman to live as a family.

Matrimony
[page 142]

_____ is the sacrament Catholics celebrate when they get married.

miracle
[page 122]

A _____ is something only God can do. It is a sign of God's love.

299

Moses
[page 158]   God chose _____ to be a leader
of God's people.

New Testament
[page 54]   The _____
is the second main part of the Bible.

Old Testament
[page 54]   The _____
is the first main part of the Bible.

Our Father
[page 226]   The _____
is the prayer Jesus taught his disciples.

Pentecost
[page 70]   _____ is the day the Holy
Spirit came to Jesus' disciples as Jesus promised.

Prayer
[page 202]   _____ is listening and talking to God.

Psalms
[page 218]   _____ are prayer songs. The
psalms the Church prays are found in the Bible.

respect
[page 174]   We show people _____ when
we love them because they are children of God.

sacraments
[page 98]

The _____ are the seven signs and celebrations of God's love that Jesus gave the Church.

saints
[page 72]

The _____ are holy people, grown-ups and children, whom the Church honors. They now live with Jesus in heaven.

Sin
[page 182]

_____ is choosing to do or say something we know is against God's laws.

Son of God
[page 30]

Jesus is the _____. Jesus is truly God and truly man.

Ten Commandments
[page 166]

The_____ are the laws God has given us to help us to live as children of God.

trust
[page 210]

To _____ someone is to believe that person will always do what is best for us.

worship
[page 166]

We _____ God when we love and honor God more than anyone and anything else.

Abraham and Sarah, 14, 38
Advent, 90, 236, 239–246
angels, 38, 39–40
Annunciation, 39–40
Ascension, 48, 279–280

Baptism, 48, 49, 71, 97–99,
    101–104, 114
believe, 14
Bible, 17, 38, 54, 115, 189
    New Testament, 54
    Old Testament, 54
    written word of God, 38
Blessed Sacrament
    and Holy Communion, 137
    name for Eucharist, 137
Blessed Teresa of Calcutta, 229

Candlemas Day, 49
candles, 49
Catholic, 70–71
Catholic Church, 17, 71
Catholic churches, naming of,
    41
children of God, 24, 133–140, 192
choices, making, 182
Christians, 77–84, 125
    as children of God, 80
    as followers of Christ, 78
    as lights in the world, 49
    first Christians, 77–83
Christmas, 30, 91, 236, 247–250
Church, 17–20, 33, 69–76
    as People of God, 70
    as community, 73, 149
    as family, 144
    beginning of, 70, 275–276
    work of, 61, 71, 73
church
    cathedrals, 169
    place of worship, 169
Church's year, 89–96, 236–282
community, 150
    belonging to 149–155
    Church as, 73,
confirmation, 98, 100
creation, 21–28
    caring for, 25, 26
    goodness of, 22

Creator, 22
cross, 46
Crucifixion, 46

D-E-F-G

deacons, 161
disciples, 46–48,
    followers of Jesus, 107–108
    women disciples, 47

Easter, 90, 92, 236, 267–280
Easter candle, 49
Eucharist, 113–114, 116, 263–264

faith, 14–16, 40, 42
    believe, 14
    gift from God, 14
    of Mary, 40
family, 16, 141–148
    as Family Church, 145
    sign of God's love, 143
family of God, 38, 144
feast days, 41
forgiveness, 46, 181–188, 259–260

Gabriel (angel), 39–40
Galilee, 122
God
    always with us, 40
    as Creator, 21–24
    laws of, 151–153
    as love, 15, 22, 38, 126
    love of, for people, 15,
        22–26,40,126–27
God the Father, 24–25, 62
God the Son. See Jesus Christ.
God the Holy Spirit. See Holy
    Spirit.
Good Friday, 265–266
Good Samaritan, 53–60
Good Shepherd, 277–278
Gospel, 55, 106–108, 115
glory, 134, 136
grace, 125
grace at meals, 205, 285
Great Commandment, 150,
    152–156

H-I-J-K

Hail Mary, 207, 283
heaven, 23, 46, 48, 72, 136,
    190–191
Holy Communion, 116–117
holy days of obligation, 93
Holy Family, 30, 31, 144
Holy Spirit, 61–68, 99–102,
    280–282
    and prayer, 206, 214
    as third Person of Trinity, 62
    as teacher and helper, 63–66,
        70
    prayer to, 67
    signs and symbols for, 65
Holy Thursday, 263–264
Holy Trinity, 62
Holy Week, 261
honor, 174
hospitals, Catholic, 57
hymns, 218, 219

image of God, 22–24, 27
Isaac, 15

Jesus Christ, 29–36, 45–52
    Ascension, 48, 279–280
    birth of, 30, 91, 236, 247–250
    burial of, 47
    childhood of, 31
    children and, 189–196
    death of, 46, 92, 265–266
    feeding people, 121–128
    forgiving people, 46
    Holy Spirit and, 63–64
    love of, for us, 45–46, 271–272
    prayer and, 203, 210, 211,
        226–227
    Resurrection, 47, 92, 267–273
    Savior, 247, 249
    Son of God, 15, 29–36, 62, 91,
        249
    the Teacher, 32, 62, 123, 167,
        178, 203–204, 209–216
    telling others about, 49–50,
        107–109
    tells us about God, 15, 24, 62,
        190, 192
    truly God and truly man, 30
John the Baptist, 241–242
Joseph, Saint, 30–31, 91, 246, 248

kindness, works of, 33
King David, 219
kingdom of God, 190–191

L-M-N-O

Last Supper, 116, 263–264
laws of God, 151–154
Lent, 90, 92, 95, 125, 236, 251–260
life, gift of, 135–139
Lord's Day, 93
love for God, 40, 42, 80, 134–136, 146
love for others, 32–34, 53–60, 64, 80, 155

marriage, 142–144
Mary, 37–44
    and Elizabeth, 243
    faith and trust of, 40, 41
    feast days of, 41
    God's love for, 41
    as greatest saint, 72
    the love of the Church for, 41
    Mother of God, 37–40
    mother of Jesus, 31, 72
Mass, 113–120
    Introductory Rites, 114, 289
    Liturgy of Eucharist, 116, 290–291
    Liturgy of Word, 115, 289
    Concluding Rites, 117, 291
Matrimony, 142
Micah the prophet, 245–246
miracle, 122–124
Moses, 157–164

Nazareth, 31
new commandment, 167
New Testament, 54

Old Testament, 54
Ordinary Time, 92, 236–238
Our Father, 21, 24, 25, 225–232

P-Q

Palm Sunday of the Lord's Passion, 261–262
parish, 17
peacemakers, 117
Pentecost, 70, 281–282

people
    as image of God, 23, 134–135
    as sharers in God's life and love, 22–23, 135
People of God, 70
pope 73, 185
prayer, 202–208, 209–216, 217–224, 225–232
    definition of, 202
    hymns, 218–221
    Jesus and, 203–204, 209–212, 226–228
    kinds of, 218–224
    learning about, 202–205
    Lent as time of, 253–254
    prayer partners, 205
    psalms, 218
    signing, 219
prayers, 283–286:
    Act of Love, 171
    Blessing prayer, 127
    Glory Prayer, 139, 283
    Hail Mary, 207, 283
    Holy Spirit, prayer to, 67
    Litany of the Saints, 75
    Litany to Jesus, 51
    Lord, have mercy, 33
    Lord's Prayer, 229
    meditation, 195
    Our Father, 25, 227, 283
    prayer of the faithful, 57, 59
    psalms, 27, 43
    Sign of Peace, 83
    Sign of the Cross, 17, 19, 62, 283
    thanksgiving, 27
    Vocation Prayer, 163, 285
priests, 99, 100, 115
prophets, 245
psalms, 218, 219

R-S-T-U

religious communities, 153
respect, showing, 32, 135, 137–138, 173, 180
Resurrection of Jesus, 47, 90, 92, 93, 269

sacraments, 98–104
saint, 72

saints
    Agnes of Assisi, 167
    Anne, 31, 72
    Catherine of Siena, 23
    Clare of Assisi, 167
    Elizabeth Ann Seton, 143
    Francis of Assisi, 109
    Joachim, 31
    John Vianney, 183
    Katharine Drexel, 135
    Martin de Porres, 81
    Mary Magdalene, 47, 269
    Patrick, 63
    Peter the Apostle, 71, 277
    Thomas the Apostle, 269
    Thérèse of Lisieux, 203
    Vincent de Paul, 175
patron saints, 81
Sarah, 14, 38
Scripture stories
    Go and Tell the Good News, 107
    Jesus and the Children, 191
    Jesus Feeds the People, 123
    Jesus Teaches Us to Pray, 211
    Joseph, 38
    Mary Magdalene, 47
    Mary, the Mother of God, 39
    Moses leads God's People, 159
    The First Christians, 79
    The Good Samaritan, 55
    The Our Father, 227
Sign of Cross, 17, 19
Sign of Peace, 185
signs and symbols, 65
sin, 46, 182–188
Son of God, 29–36

tabernacle, 137
Ten Commandments, 165–172, 173–176
Triduum, 263–268
trust, 40, 158
truth, telling, 176

V-W-X-Y-Z

vocation, 163
word of God, 38
worship, 166–172
worship, Church's year of, 89–96, 235–282